T0209720

An Analysis of

John Stuart Mill's

On Liberty

Ashleigh Campi
with
Lindsay Scorgie-Porter

Published by Macat International Ltd
24:13 Coda Centre, 189 Munster Road, London SW6 6AW.

Distributed exclusively by Routledge
2 Park Square, Milton Park, Abingdon, Oxon OX14 4RN
711 Third Avenue, New York, NY 10017, USA

Routledge is an imprint of the Taylor & Francis Group, an informa business

www.macat.com
info@macat.com

Cataloguing in Publication Data
A catalogue record for this book is available from the British Library.
Library of Congress Cataloguing-in-Publication Data is available upon request.
Cover illustration: Etienne Gilfillan

ISBN 978-1-912303-38-0 (hardback)
ISBN 978-1-912127-20-7 (paperback)
ISBN 978-1-912282-26-5 (e-book)

Notice

CONTENTS

THE MACAT LIBRARY

The Macat Library is a series of unique academic explorations of seminal works in the humanities and social sciences – books and papers that have had a significant and widely recognised impact on their disciplines. It has been created to serve as much more than just a summary of what lies between the covers of a great book. It illuminates and explores the influences on, ideas of, and impact of that book. Our goal is to offer a learning resource that encourages critical thinking and fosters a better, deeper understanding of important ideas.

Each publication is divided into three Sections: Influences, Ideas, and Impact. Each Section has four Modules. These explore every important facet of the work, and the responses to it.

This Section-Module structure makes a Macat Library book easy to use, but it has another important feature. Because each Macat book is written to the same format, it is possible (and encouraged!) to cross-reference multiple Macat books along the same lines of inquiry or research. This allows the reader to open up interesting interdisciplinary pathways.

To further aid your reading, lists of glossary terms and people mentioned are included at the end of this book (these are indicated by an asterisk [*] throughout) – as well as a list of works cited.

Macat has worked with the University of Cambridge to identify the elements of critical thinking and understand the ways in which six different skills combine to enable effective thinking.
Three allow us to fully understand a problem; three more give us the tools to solve it. Together, these six skills make up the **PACIER** model of critical thinking. They are:

ANALYSIS – understanding how an argument is built
EVALUATION – exploring the strengths and weaknesses of an argument
INTERPRETATION – understanding issues of meaning

CREATIVE THINKING – coming up with new ideas and fresh connections
PROBLEM-SOLVING – producing strong solutions
REASONING – creating strong arguments

To find out more, visit **WWW.MACAT.COM.**

CRITICAL THINKING AND *ON LIBERTY*

Primary critical thinking skill: INTERPRETATION
Secondary critical thinking skill: REASONING

In his wonderfully clear and cogent essay *On Liberty*, Mill contends that individuals should be as free as possible from interference by government. Proposing that individual fulfilment is the surest route to collective happiness, he argues passionately against the "tyranny of the majority," and sets out to create an alternative view of a practical politics that sets proper limits on the powers of government and society.

The result, Mill argues, will be not only greater freedom, but also improved social progress. He reached these conclusions by re-interpreting a large body of existing political and philosophical thought – introducing insights drawn from several different schools of thought, and thereby creating an unparalleled defense of classic liberal principals. Much of the clarity of thought that Mill has become celebrated for is the product of his ability to explain meaning, define terms, and highlight problems and issues of definition – making him an exemplar of high quality interpretive thinking

ABOUT THE AUTHOR OF THE ORIGINAL WORK

Son of Scottish philosopher James Mill, the philosopher and economist **John Stuart Mill** was a child prodigy who learned Greek at three, Latin at eight, and was studying political economy at 13. Unsurprisingly, he suffered a nervous breakdown at 20, but recovered to continue working for the famous East India Company, and later become a Liberal Member of Parliament. Mill was one of the first people to demand the right to vote for women, backed a number of social reforms, and helped define concepts of freedom in his writing. He died in 1873 in France.

ABOUT THE AUTHORS OF THE ANALYSIS

Dr Ashleigh Campi is visiting lecturer in the Department of Politics at Scripps College. She holds a PhD in political science from the University of Chicago.

Dr Lindsay Scorgie Porter is visiting assistant professor in politics at the University of Western Ontario. She holds a PhD in politics and international studies from the University of Cambridge and an MSc in global politics from the London School of Economics.

ABOUT MACAT

GREAT WORKS FOR CRITICAL THINKING

Macat is focused on making the ideas of the world's great thinkers accessible and comprehensible to everybody, everywhere, in ways that promote the development of enhanced critical thinking skills.

It works with leading academics from the world's top universities to produce new analyses that focus on the ideas and the impact of the most influential works ever written across a wide variety of academic disciplines. Each of the works that sit at the heart of its growing library is an enduring example of great thinking. But by setting them in context – and looking at the influences that shaped their authors, as well as the responses they provoked – Macat encourages readers to look at these classics and game-changers with fresh eyes. Readers learn to think, engage and challenge their ideas, rather than simply accepting them.

'Macat offers an amazing first-of-its-kind tool for interdisciplinary learning and research. Its focus on works that transformed their disciplines and its rigorous approach, drawing on the world's leading experts and educational institutions, opens up a world-class education to anyone.'

Andreas Schleicher
Director for Education and Skills, Organisation for Economic
Co-operation and Development

'Macat is taking on some of the major challenges in university education ... They have drawn together a strong team of active academics who are producing teaching materials that are novel in the breadth of their approach.'

Prof Lord Broers,
former Vice-Chancellor of the University of Cambridge

'The Macat vision is exceptionally exciting. It focuses upon new modes of learning which analyse and explain seminal texts which have profoundly influenced world thinking and so social and economic development. It promotes the kind of critical thinking which is essential for any society and economy.
This is the learning of the future.'

Rt Hon Charles Clarke, former UK Secretary of State for Education

'The Macat analyses provide immediate access to the critical conversation surrounding the books that have shaped their respective discipline, which will make them an invaluable resource to all of those, students and teachers, working in the field.'

Professor William Tronzo, University of California at San Diego

WAYS IN TO THE TEXT

KEY POINTS

- John Stuart Mill was a nineteenth-century philosopher and politician who set out an enormously influential definition of individual freedom in a liberal* democracy.

- *On Liberty* attempts to answer the central and enduring question of how much power society should have to interfere in the life of the individual.

- Mill's ideas remain relevant today as modern thinkers grapple with understanding liberty in an age of social media, competing definitions of freedom and the resurgence of religion in politics.

Who Was John Stuart Mill?

John Stuart Mill was a nineteenth-century philosopher and political thinker whose ideas remain central to our understanding of the world's liberal democracies—those states with governments that guarantee to respect the freedoms of their citizens.

Mill was born in 1806 into a London family that moved in influential intellectual circles. His father, the Scottish philosopher James Mill, followed the school of thought known as "utilitarianism";* he believed, that is, that an action should be judged right if it led to happiness, and wrong if it led to unhappiness.

Mill was educated under an unrelenting regime devised by his father, taught ancient Greek from the age of three and forbidden friendships. This difficult childhood took a toll, however, and Mill suffered a breakdown at the age of 20. Turning to the Romantic* poets and thinkers, he combined utilitarianism with Romantic ideas of art and beauty to create an original theory about what it means to be free.

His works include *A System of Logic* (1843), *Principles of Political Economy* (1848), *Utilitarianism, Considerations on Representative Government* (both 1861), and *The Subjection of Women* (1869)—but by far the most famous is *On Liberty* (1859).

Mill fell in love with a married woman, Harriet Hardy Taylor, and had to wait 20 years until she was free to marry him in 1851. In 1858 Taylor died suddenly while helping Mill to edit *On Liberty,* which he published the following year.

He retired from the East India Company,* where he had worked since he was 17, and moved to France to write and tend Taylor's grave. Mill returned to England in 1865 as a member of Parliament and an outspoken critic of slavery. He died at the age of 66 in Avignon, and was laid to rest with his wife.

What Does *On Liberty* Say?

John Stuart Mill sets out to answer one of the most difficult and enduring questions in Western thought: what exactly does it mean to be a free person in a free society?

On Liberty immediately lays bare the problem at the center of Mill's argument—where to draw the line over how much say everyone else has in what we can do. Mill's defense of civil liberty* rests, in his own words, on the need to define the "nature and limits of the power which can be legitimately exercised by society over the individual."

Mill's benchmark for deciding what counts as legitimate interference from the state or other members of society is called the "harm principle":* the state or society can only exercise power over a person if that person's behavior would cause harm to another person or group. It is not enough just to claim interference is for someone's "own good."

Central to Mill's classical liberal approach is freedom of speech: the idea that we should be able to express any of our opinions in public without being censored by the government. Opinions should not be banned, he argues, because the only way for good ideas to survive and bad ones to fail is to test them in open debate. And with free speech, according to *On Liberty*, comes the right to turn thoughts into action.

Protecting our freedom to live and think as we choose requires vigilance, and Mill details where the main threats to liberty lie. *On Liberty*, a stout defense of everyone's right to think differently, warns against the "tyranny of the majority"—which becomes a problem when freedom is not threatened by legal force but, rather, by the sheer weight of popular opinion. The majority can easily smother minority opinions and disapprove of life choices, and individuality must be protected against this threat.

A strong theme running through *On Liberty* is that individuality is supremely valuable, both to personal happiness and by allowing progress toward the wisdom that can lead us, collectively, to a better society. This element of Mill's theory has real resonance for modern thinkers and politicians as they grapple with the impact on individuals of new forms of mass media such as Twitter, Facebook and YouTube, which can very quickly mobilize mass approval or disapproval.

On Liberty is not a perfect blueprint for liberal democracy. After all, no single scholar has all the answers. One unanswered problem is the nature of the balance that needs to be struck between individual freedom under the "harm principle" and the state's obligation to ensure social justice.* Some readers also see a certain snobbishness in Mill's insistence that only a cultured elite can lead the way to a more evolved society.

Nevertheless, *On Liberty* is a passionate plea for a tolerant society in which everyone is free to live as they wish within a safe, ethical, and orderly community. The book, written in 1859, still contains some of the bedrock principles for liberal democracies across the world.

Why Does *On Liberty* Matter?

Scholars and political thinkers will always need *On Liberty* if they are properly to understand the history of Western thought behind the global success of liberal democracy in the nineteenth, twentieth, and early twenty-first centuries. But Mill's landmark book also has a more practical role. The issues we grapple with today were present when Mill was writing in the late 1800s and he identifies essential questions that each generation has had to answer for itself.

In a world of seven billion people, where nations and regions are endlessly combining or splintering, there are many powerful and competing definitions of freedom. Just as Mill was writing amid the social upheaval of industrialization, modern scholars must take on the shifts in world power as a result of the Cold War* and the impact of the digital age. *On Liberty* is a useful starting point for new debate around what we mean by individual and collective freedom—and its repercussions for how we live our lives today.

Mill's ideas on the rights of women are especially significant. Radical* for their time, they are still pertinent to the ongoing fight for gender equality across the world. Mill's wider calls for an end to slavery have modern echoes in the fight to end the misery of human trafficking. His worry about mass opinion silencing those who think or act differently is alive in the challenge of social media. "Well-being" and "mindfulness" are modern buzzwords for achieving human wisdom—but they are new names for what Mill described in his defense of individuality and human "flourishing."

This is not to say that John Stuart Mill was "right." In fact, it is not necessary to agree with anything *On Liberty* has to say—it is a fact that the work triggered an important and continuing debate on the fundamental issues around what constitutes freedom, truth, security, and personal happiness. For a century and a half, Mill's rules on personal freedom and the limits of state control were a powerful part of political thinking as liberal democracy spread around the globe.

However, fundamental shifts in power in recent decades have opened a whole new debate over how society should be organized. The world has been rocked by events such as the terrorist attack on the Twin Towers in New York City of 2001; revelations about the extent of Internet state monitoring of individuals and the use of torture for political ends; the chaos following the wars in Iraq; murders triggered by cartoons seen as offensive to Islam; and the growing role of religion in political action.

As the world copes with a new era of revolution and social upheaval it is useful to understand Mill's defense of a certain dominant view of freedom—and to decide whether it still applies in today's world.

SECTION 1
INFLUENCES

THE AUTHOR AND THE HISTORICAL CONTEXT

KEY POINTS

- *On Liberty* remains a highly regarded text because it sets out clearly the classic liberal* principles that underpin democracies.

- John Stuart Mill was hugely influenced by his father, the Scottish philosopher and political economist James Mill,* who took personal charge of his son's grueling education.

- Mill's landmark book was written amid debates raging among Victorian thinkers over the hope for and nature of progress in a time of political and social upheaval.

Why Read This Text?

John Stuart Mill's *On Liberty* has stood the test of time. As the Australian scholar Andrew Norton* points out, "John Stuart Mill is the only nineteenth-century liberal intellectual still widely read and discussed in the twenty-first century, thanks mainly to his book *On Liberty*."[1]

Mill is among the most influential thinkers of the liberal tradition and *On Liberty* has been hailed as "the most passionate treatise on human freedom ever written."[2] He brings together various strands of radical* thought about how society works to create an original and detailed defense of the individual. The book is still valued by scholars and politicians for its clear description and defense of classic liberal principles.

At its heart is a question that many places in the world continue to struggle to answer: what is the best balance to strike between the freedom of the individual and the needs of society?

> ❝ The subject of this Essay is not the so-called Liberty of the Will, so unfortunately opposed to the misnamed doctrine of Philosophical Necessity; but Civil, or Social Liberty: the nature and limits of the power which can be legitimately exercised by society over the individual. ❞
>
> John Stuart Mill, *On Liberty*

Part of the enduring appeal of *On Liberty* is Mill's eccentric and wide-ranging intellectual style. He embraces the concerns both of analytically minded followers of utilitarianism* (the philosophy of using "utility"* to calculate what counts as morally and socially good, according to which an action is right if it tends to promote happiness, and wrong if it does not) and poets and literary critics more focused on beauty and emotion. The result is a powerful and enduring argument for the value of individualism that speaks to people with a variety of outlooks, interests, and political beliefs.

Author's Life

Mill was born in 1806 in London, England, and grew up in an academic hothouse. His father was the Scottish philosopher and economist James Mill, who was determined to raise a genius through an education that began with the teaching of Greek at the age of three. This intensive tutoring was profoundly influenced by the elder Mill's friendship with the philosopher Jeremy Bentham,* founder of the school of utilitarianism.[3]

Mill was surrounded by famous philosophers from childhood and enjoyed debate with radical thinkers all his life, especially the French philosopher Auguste Comte* and the Scottish philosopher Thomas Carlyle.* At 14, Mill moved to France to study, living with Bentham's brother. When he returned home he rejected the universities of

Oxford and Cambridge; both were affiliated to the Church of England,* and as an atheist* he refused to accept religious rules over his studies. So at 17 he went to work as a clerk for the British East India Company* and attended classes in ethics and law by the utilitarian philosopher John Austin*[4] at University College London.

The pressures of Mill's childhood caught up with him at 20 when he suffered a nervous breakdown; he turned to art and poetry during his recovery and began to question the utilitarian philosophy in which he had been raised.

He published *A System of Logic* in 1843 and *Principles of Political Economy* in 1848. Three years later he married his fellow philosopher Harriet Hardy Taylor, a longtime friend and intellectual collaborator. Exactly how much influence she had on Mill's philosophy is still debated; Nicholas Capaldi, Mill's biographer, argues that although Taylor did not provide her husband with new ideas, she did help him clarify his thoughts.[5]

Taylor helped to edit *On Liberty* and in his *Autobiography* (1874) Mill says they planned to go to the south of Europe to complete the final draft of the book. However, she died suddenly in 1858; so in 1859 Mill published the last version they had worked on together.

After losing his job with the winding up of the East India Company, Mill moved to the city of Avignon in France, where he continued to write. *Utilitarianism* and *Considerations on Representative Government* were published in 1861. In 1869 he wrote *The Subjection of Women* with the help of his stepdaughter, the women's rights activist Helen Taylor.*

Mill returned to England in 1865 and was elected as a member of the British Parliament, acting as a radical voice on issues such as slavery, colonization, and equal rights. He died aged 66 in 1873 in Avignon and was buried there alongside his wife.

Author's Background

On Liberty was the product of an intellectual battlefield on which nineteenth-century scholars fought to give shape and meaning to social change in the decades following the French* and American revolutions.* Debate centered on theories of what can prompt society to change for the better.

Mill was deeply involved with the work of parliamentary radicals to reform the electoral system and the utilitarian school of his father, and was influenced by the poetry and literary theory of the English Romantic* movement through the works of the writer Carlyle and the poets Samuel Taylor Coleridge* and William Wordsworth.* He was also influenced by the utopian ideas of progress, industry, and socialism of the Saint-Simonian* school, based on the thought of the French philosopher Claude Henri de Rouvroy,* and by his colleague Auguste Comte.

Romantic individualism took the position that a cultivated elite could guide social progress. Comte believed that it was possible for a society to find that its political and social arrangements did not match with the opinions and beliefs of its people. At this point, certain individuals would step into the gap between the two to shake up the social order. Leading by example, they would introduce new beliefs, practices, tastes, and understanding.

For Saint-Simonians (and for Romantics such as Coleridge) these educated and visionary people, who saw beyond the cultural limits of their age, were the key to improving society.

These ideas all had an impact on Mill and were the background to the theories he set out in *On Liberty*.

NOTES

1   Andrew Norton, "*On Liberty* at 150," *Policy* 25.2 (2009), 49.

2   Christopher Clausen, "John Stuart Mill's 'Very Simple Principle,'" *The Wilson Quarterly* 33.2 (2009), 40.

3   Wendy Donner and Richard A. Fumerton, *Mill* (Chichester: Wiley-Blackwell, 2009).

4   Austin's attempt to separate positive law* from moral rules may have inspired Mill's attention to both the moral force of popular opinion and, distinctly, the force of legal coercion as two forms of social interference in individual thought and action.

5   Anthony Skelton, "Liberty's godfather," *The Globe and Mail*, May 20, 2006.

MODULE 2
ACADEMIC CONTEXT

KEY POINTS

- Political philosophy in John Stuart Mill's era was concerned with how much influence the government should have in the life of an individual.

- Attempts to answer this core question date back at least to the seventeenth century and *Leviathan*, a classic work by the philosopher Thomas Hobbes.*

- *On Liberty* defended individual liberty by describing the role of independent and creative self-development in social progress.

The Work in its Context

John Stuart Mill wrote *On Liberty* in the England of the 1850s—a nation coming to terms with its rapid industrialization. A central debate within political philosophy concerned the development of policy in the wake of the social and economic upheaval of the Industrial Revolution.* Debate within the fields of political economy* (the relationship between politics and economics) and legal and social theory in particular revolved around the demands of a newly industrialized society.

Industrialization transformed the lives of many with the rapid growth of cities swollen by migration from the countryside, increasing rural and urban poverty, and the emergence of the urban working and middle classes. Philosophers, statesmen, intellectuals, and jurists, attempting to respond to these changes, argued over how much involvement the government should have in an individual's life.

Industrialization brought a growing problem of poverty, which was addressed by utilitarians* with a critique of social assistance

> **❝** The only freedom which deserves the name is that of pursuing our own good in our own way, so long as we do not attempt to deprive others of theirs, or impede their efforts to obtain it. **❞**
>
> John Stuart Mill, *On Liberty*

programs such as the English Poor Laws.* These laws sparked great debate when they were reformed in 1834. The new rules gave the government the power to set up workhouses designed to put the unemployed urban poor to work. This was a substantial shift away from the previous laws, which provided help for those in need without forcing them to work.[1] The Poor Laws were a key issue in discussions about the limit of social authority over the individual. The social conditions of industrialization and economic development also brought the issue of education to the forefront of public debate.

Overview of the Field

The proper limits of government power have preoccupied political thinkers since at least the seventeenth century, when the English philosopher Thomas Hobbes wrote *Leviathan* (1651). He argues that to avoid a short and violent life, people need to enter into a social contract* to accept a central authority. This is considered to be the first work to tackle the question of the fair limits of state power over a person. In the century that followed, liberalism* became a doctrine that advocated limiting state intervention in private affairs. Liberal thinkers who attempted to pin down exactly where these limits lay included the philosopher John Locke,* who established the principles of limited government based on the protection of private property. The idea that natural economic laws function independently of state action[2] came from the British economists Thomas Malthus,* David Ricardo,* and Adam Smith.*

The whole issue of what Mill calls "social liberty"* was of central importance in classical liberalism. Demands for individual freedom came largely from a growing middle class made up of merchants, capitalists, financiers, and other professionals who wanted to curb royal and aristocratic power over trade and commerce. The backdrop of religious conflict between Roman Catholic and Protestant Christians across Europe in the wake of the Reformation* added urgency to the debate.

Academic Influences

Mill's ideas were shaped by growing up among some of the most influential thinkers of his day, including his father and teacher James Mill.* Andrew Norton,* a scholar of education, describes the program designed by Mill's father as "the most crushing educational workload ever imposed on a child."[3] The young Mill familiarized himself with the economic arguments of Smith and Ricardo, and undertook an extensive study of the major works of the Greek philosopher Aristotle.*

James Mill was part of a circle known as the "philosophical radicals"* with thinkers such as Jeremy Bentham*—the founder of utilitarianism, the idea that right actions bring happiness and wrong ones bring unhappiness.

Mill was trained by his father and by Bentham, but as he entered his twenties he suffered a serious bout of depression and questioned how he had been taught to think. The rationality of utilitarianism had its limits and Mill began to engage with more emotional approaches to understanding life. He turned to the Romantic* poets William Wordsworth* and Samuel Taylor Coleridge;* the influence of their work can be seen in his emphasis on the importance of individual creativity.

When Mill discovered the work of the French philosopher Auguste Comte,* he began what would become an extensive correspondence. Though Mill considered Comte to be obsessed with morality (in his description, a "morality-intoxicated man") he was influenced by Comte's account of history being driven by periods of social and cultural innovation.[4]

All these influences had a bearing on Mill's version of personal freedom described in *On Liberty.* The text was highly original for its day and added to the classic defense of individual liberty by emphasizing the role of creative self-development in improving society. Personal tastes, preferences, and opinions lead to progress if they are arrived at freely through open discussion and experimentation. This echoes Coleridge's belief that culturally educated people drive change.

NOTES

1   Karl Polanyi, *The Great Transformation: The Political and Economic Origins of Our Times* (Boston: Beacon Press, 2001).

2   Works central to the early development of classical political economy include: Thomas Malthus, *An Essay on the Principle of Population* (1798–1826); David Ricardo, *Principles of Political Economy and Taxation* (1817); and Adam Smith, *An Inquiry into the Nature and Causes of the Wealth of Nations* (1776).

3   Andrew Norton, "*On Liberty* at 150," *Policy* 25.2 (2009), 51.

4   Ben Eggleston et al., eds., *John Stuart Mill and the Art of Life* (Oxford: Oxford University Press, 2011), 10.

MODULE 3
THE PROBLEM

KEY POINTS

- John Stuart Mill's core concern was liberty—especially how much power it was reasonable for society to have over individuals.

- In common with the philosophers Thomas Hobbes* and John Locke,* Mill describes liberty in terms of limiting state interference in people's lives.

- *On Liberty* was original and radical* because it argued that personal freedom leads to new and improved tastes, ideas, and ways of life.

Core Question

John Stuart Mill tackles the nature of personal freedom in a modern society head on. In the first paragraph, he sets out the big question that *On Liberty* is designed to answer: to identify "the nature and limits of the power which can be legitimately exercised by society over the individual."[1]

Mill provides an answer using concepts that have fueled the debate over individual freedom versus state control ever since.

On Liberty addresses both the concerns of economic liberalism and issues of religious toleration. Following the philosophers Thomas Hobbes and John Locke, Mill frames the issue of social liberty* in terms of limitations on state power; all three thinkers conceived of social liberty, tied to the exercise of reason, as driving social progress.

Mill also links the defense of liberty to the recognition of human reason, as thinkers from the Enlightenment*—who championed thought over authority—did before him.

❝ The struggle between Liberty and Authority is the most conspicuous feature in the portions of history with which we are earliest familiar, particularly in that of Greece, Rome, and England. **❞**

John Stuart Mill, *On Liberty*

Mill's defense of liberty offers an original case for how individualism can play a crucial and productive role in the moral side of human progress. He argues that individual liberty leads people to new and potentially superior ways of living and thinking. This radically progressive strand in Mill sets him apart from the liberal* tradition he inherited.

The Participants

On Liberty can be seen in terms of the philosophical shift away from the mechanistic* view of society (according to which society functions like a machine, made of individual "components" that together complete a social whole) of the seventeenth and eighteenth centuries towards the organicist* theory (according to which society functions like a natural organism, made of organic "wholes") popular in the nineteenth century when Mill was writing.

The mechanistic method examines society by looking at the forces and actions of its parts, which are human beings. One understands how society works by explaining the behavior of individuals who relate to one another to form the whole. The views of both Mill's father and the philosopher Jeremy Bentham* on liberalism and political economy were grounded in this interpretation of society. This was the worldview in which they educated Mill, hoping their protégé would become the next great champion of their utilitarian* theory.

Organicists, by contrast, understand society by examining social institutions and social relations. They home in on the impact that particular historical forms of thought and order have had on shaping human nature. The French philosopher Auguste Comte* and the German philosopher G.W. F. Hegel* are among the prominent figures associated with organicist views.

Although Mill rejects the mechanistic view of society, he does not follow other social philosophers of his day in adopting the organicist view wholesale. In *On Liberty*, he instead examines elements of both.

The Contemporary Debate

It is commonly accepted by scholars that Mill was strongly influenced by Auguste Comte, his friend and correspondent over many years. During his shift away from orthodox utilitarianism as a young man, Mill studied Comte and the Saint-Simonian* school (an intellectual movement based on the progressive ideas of the French philosopher Claude Henri de Rouvroy),* commenting on their theories in *Westminster Review.*

Mill also accepts the challenge to his early utilitarian ideas about government from the British politician T. B. Macaulay.* It was not possible to derive laws of social order merely from laws of human nature, according to Macaulay; historical and cultural conditions must be taken into account. Mill answers these criticisms in *On Liberty* in a way that is influenced by, but ultimately different from, the views of Comte.

Mill can be seen as claiming the middle ground in the enduring debate over what drives society forward. He walks a line between those who concentrate on individuals and those who emphasize the role of institutions in shaping human destiny. On the one hand, Mill stands among the social theorists who acknowledge the importance of social groupings on shaping our nature. On the other hand, he values the basic characteristics of our thought and individual creative powers that are common to any age.

NOTES

1   John Stuart Mill, *On Liberty* (New York: Dover Publications, 2002), 1.

MODULE 4
THE AUTHOR'S CONTRIBUTION

KEY POINTS

- John Stuart Mill develops the theory of the principle of utility*—that a right action adds to happiness and a wrong one does not—to accommodate different paths to individual freedom and therefore social progress.

- At the heart of *On Liberty* is Mill's "harm principle,"* according to which interference in individual liberty can only be justified if one person's actions will harm the interests of someone else.

- Mill draws on the theories of British and German Romanticism,* British utilitarianism,* and liberalism* to make an original case for liberty.

Author's Aims

John Stuart Mill uses *On Liberty* to argue that individuals should be as free as possible from their government telling them what to think and do. His earlier work rested on the utilitarian philosophy developed by his father James Mill* and Jeremy Bentham.* According to this philosophy, "utility" is the measure of right and wrong. An action is right if it promotes happiness and wrong if it does the opposite.

The philosopher T. B. Macaulay* criticized this vision of social order, saying it ignores the realities of history and culture. Mill answers Macaulay in *On Liberty* with a notion of freedom that includes many roads to personal fulfillment, depending on circumstances, all meeting at a set of higher pleasures and reasoned truths.

On Liberty contains major revisions to utilitarianism. Mill rejects the calculation that expects individual pleasure to converge in the greatest general happiness. Instead Mill offers a passionate defense of an active,

> 66 The will of the people, moreover, practically means the will of the most numerous or the most active part of the people; the majority, or those who succeed in making themselves accepted as the majority; the people, consequently, may desire to oppress a part of their number; and precautions are as much needed against this as against any other abuse of power. 99

John Stuart Mill, *On Liberty*

holistic view of individual fulfillment that leads to general happiness. Happiness can come from lives made up of different opinions and behavior. So given that human happiness is complicated, we can expect people to choose different paths to achieving such fulfillment. Mill insists that such diversity should be protected because it is essential to individual happiness. His passion for protecting individuality follows from the idea of the "tyranny of the majority" made famous by the French political theorist and writer Alexis de Tocqueville,* according to which popular opinion can stifle minority ideas.

On Liberty is devoted to weaving these new ideas into classical utilitarianism and exploring what they mean for politics. Mill largely achieves his aims. He tackles the problem of the tyranny of the majority on the progress of knowledge. He devotes a section to the role of individuality in achieving well-being and examines the implications of his theories for governing society.

Approach

Mill was raised as a utilitarian by his father James Mill, and *On Liberty* reflects how that philosophy affected his attempt to work out what is best for society. The crux of the book is Mill's "harm principle": interference in individual liberty can only be justified when a person's actions will harm another's interests.

The harm principle states that "the sole end for which mankind are warranted, individually or collectively, in interfering with the liberty of action of any of their number, is self-protection. That the only purpose for which power can be rightfully exercised over any member of a civilized community, against his will, is to prevent harm to others. His own good, either physical or moral, is not a sufficient warrant."[1]

The scholar Andrew Norton notes that "Mill's harm principle … may be 'very simple' to state, but its application is complex, as his own examples, and a large secondary literature over the last century and a half, show."[2]

Mill parts company with orthodox utilitarianism in *On Liberty* when he includes ideas from the Romantic* movement. He was influenced by the poet Samuel Taylor Coleridge,* who explored the importance of emotion and aesthetic experience in our private or "inner" life. Wilhelm von Humboldt,* the Prussian philosopher, is also referred to throughout *On Liberty*. From him, Mill took the idea that human uniqueness is an essential source of social progress.

Classical utilitarianism views happiness in terms of pleasures and positive sensation. Mill sees it as tied to the individual's free development of a life suited to his or her particular talents and ideas. "Where other people's traditions, rather than the person's own character, are the rule of conduct, Mill thought that there is 'wanting one of the principal ingredients of human happiness,'" explains Norton.[3]

Contribution in Context

Mill defends the role of individualism by drawing together strands of overlapping philosophical theory in mid-nineteenth century Europe. He does not confine himself to any one school of thought and *On Liberty* builds on the ideas of British and German Romanticism, British utilitarianism, and liberalism to create a compelling new theory.

It is easy to overlook just how original Mill's version of political liberalism is in the philosophy of human rights. This is because *On*

Liberty is part of a well-trodden path of classical political and economic thought most often associated with the work of the Enlightenment* thinker John Locke.*

Locke's famous *Two Treatises of Government* (1689) and *A Letter Concerning Toleration* (1689) became the basis of liberal theory by describing how society can allow people to live as they choose. Locke set out the individual right to earn a living and pursue happiness through state protection of both private property and personal opinion. This means different beliefs should be tolerated without interference by a government or other individuals.

Mill puts a novel twist on the basic tenets of liberal thought, arguing that individual freedom is crucial to the moral dimension of social progress. Arguing that individual liberty leads to a superior kind of life sets Mill apart from the liberal tradition he inherited.

NOTES

1   John Stuart Mill, *On Liberty* (New York: Dover Publications, 2002), 8.

2   Andrew Norton, "*On Liberty* at 150," *Policy* 25.2 (2009), 50.

3   Norton, "*On Liberty*," 50.

SECTION 2
IDEAS

MAIN IDEAS

KEY POINTS

- In *On Liberty*, John Stuart Mill describes individual freedom, including the need to guard against the tyranny of the majority, and defines the proper limits on the power of government and society to interfere in our lives.

- The work explains the forms this power can take and the nature of the threat it poses to freedom—and therefore social progress.

- Mill brings fresh insights drawn from several schools of thought to create an unprecedented defense of classic liberal* principles.

Key Themes

John Stuart Mill has an ambitious mission for *On Liberty*—he wants to define the very nature of personal freedom by defining the exact "nature and limits of the power which can be legitimately exercised by society over the individual."[1] In making his passionate and enduring case, Mill focuses on issues at the very heart of his notion of liberty.

The overarching concern of *On Liberty* is how much reach society should have into the life of an individual. To answer this question Mill seeks to clarify the nature and use of power, especially when it threatens our freedom to live as we choose. He does this through an exploration of the themes of freedom of speech and action, the tyranny of the majority, the value of individuality, and the need to limit government interference.

The test he applies to all these is the "harm principle,"* which he explains as follows: "The sole end for which mankind are warranted,

> **❝** The object of this essay is to assert one very simple principle, as entitled to govern absolutely the dealings of society with the individual in the way of compulsion and control, whether the means used be physical force in the form of legal penalties, or the moral coercion of public opinion. **❞**
>
> John Stuart Mill, *On Liberty*

individually or collectively in interfering with the liberty of action of any of their number, is self-protection. That the only purpose for which power can be rightfully exercised over any member of a civilized community, against his will, is to prevent harm to others. His own good, either physical or moral, is not a sufficient warrant."[2]

Exploring the Ideas

Freedom of speech is a guiding principle in liberal thought. Mill's work is no exception.

He defends the right of people to express their opinions (spoken and written) in public without being censored by the government. His argument for this is simple. Open discussion means that ideas are subject to reasoned criticism and so improve over time. Mill argues for freedom of action with the more radical* claim that free expression of ideas cannot be separated from freedom to turn them into action.

Of course, free thought and action can be stopped with either legal force by the government, or moral constraint from society through popular opinion. This is where Mill reminds us of the "tyranny of the majority," an undesirable state of affairs which comes into effect when popular opinion quashes minority views, beliefs, and lifestyles through widespread disapproval. This is a powerful force because most people have to be accepted by society in order to earn a living; departing too radically from the views of the majority puts their livelihoods at risk.

On Liberty sounds a warning against allowing mainstream society to snuff out ideas and lifestyle experiments in this way. Mill argues that the expression of minority opinions—and progressive tastes that swim against the popular tide—are at constant risk of being stifled. This is a very serious risk to the health of society, Mill suggests, as he makes the case that individuality is an essential part of human well-being.

Language and Expression
On Liberty is noted for the clarity of the writing Mill uses to convey his original and influential theory. His passionate language and style bear little resemblance to the intellectual schools that Mill engaged in debate. He combines elements of these movements with his own theories to call for a tolerant society in which everyone is free to live as they wish.

Perhaps the most innovative use of language in *On Liberty* comes during the discussion of individuality. While Mill was inspired by Wilhelm von Humboldt,* his vision moves beyond that of the Prussian theorist. Reflecting on the struggles of figures from history lends weight to Mill's arguments. So he holds up as examples great individuals who fought to bring new ideas into the world, including Jesus Christ and the Greek philosopher Socrates.* Each of these people, Mill reminds the reader, suffered persecution at the hands of a hostile public that did not want to see established ideas challenged.

Mill also builds a sense of urgency by taking a close look at the quality of government in his day, and the "lovers of liberty" who defend political and civil rights. The text sometimes reads like a political manifesto, giving the impression that he is tackling issues where the stakes are high.

Mill argues for social liberty by engaging with new schools of thought and responding to his critics. *On Liberty* also contains literary reflections on the depth of individual experience, accounts of progress through reasoned debate, the utilitarian logic of general happiness, and the liberal defense of free speech and action. By all these means, Mill arrives at a novel and enduring defense of classical liberal principles.

NOTES

1   John Stuart Mill, *On Liberty* (New York: Dover Publications, 2002), 1.

2   Mill, *On Liberty*, 8.

MODULE 6
SECONDARY IDEAS

KEY POINTS

- John Stuart Mill offers secondary ideas derived from the nineteenth-century debate about human nature and the use of reason.

- Mill's theory of the progress of knowledge is key to his central themes, such as freedom of speech.

- The work's secondary ideas help to make *On Liberty* an innovative text for its day.

Other Ideas

On Liberty sets out John Stuart Mill's belief that individuality is essential to human well-being and must be defended using the "harm principle."* But it is important to pay close attention to the other ideas Mill brings into play to support the thrust of his main argument.

The most important minor themes at work in *On Liberty* come from the ideas being debated by Mill's fellow philosophers and other scholars in the early nineteenth century. The progressive idea of human nature grounded in the use of reason is the cornerstone of Enlightenment* thought. (The Enlightenment was a period of intense cultural, political and intellectual development of the mid-seventeenth to the eighteenth century.)

Put simply, the idea is that we are able to perfect our knowledge of the world over time by using our ability to reason.

Reason (according to this strand of Enlightenment thought) is put to work through the method of systematic inquiry that emerged in the scientific revolution*—a period from about 1550 to the late eighteenth century, marked by the emergence of modern science. The

> ❝ Every man who says frankly and fully what he thinks is so far doing a public service. We should be grateful to him for attacking most unsparingly our most cherished opinions. ❞
>
> John Stuart Mill, *On Liberty*

scientific method tests theories against organized observations to improve existing ideas. In this way, human knowledge progresses over time.

This concept of progressive knowledge informs the whole of *On Liberty*, especially Mill's defense of free speech. Mill agrees with John Milton,* who in *Areopagitica* (1644) also argued that censoring new or unusual ideas makes open debate impossible.

Open debate forces us to defend opinions and beliefs by giving explanations of how we arrived at them. False opinions are exposed and true opinions are strengthened by their defense against opposing views. Free discussion is the motor of progress in two senses. First, it allows for the improvement of ideas; second, taking part in free discussion improves our ability to evaluate arguments and judge the quality of ideas.

Exploring the Ideas

On Liberty builds on established thought to present nineteenth-century scholars with a fresh approach to the most enduring themes.

Mill starts by defending the open expression of different opinions and beliefs. He moves on to defend the fact that people have a range of preferences and may choose to try out many things in their lives. He points to areas of life in which human diversity is a good thing. These include our tastes and pursuits and the many ways we act together with others. Mill argues that we are all unique individuals and this range of ways of life and belief is an inevitable result of individuality.

He insists that human diversity has a crucial role to play in the progressive development of human ways of life.

At this point, a difficulty emerges in Mill's thought that can be understood as both an innovation as well as a challenge to later thinkers.

Mill moves away from the simplistic idea of human happiness advanced by the older generation of utilitarian* liberals who suggest that individual interests converge on general happiness. He challenges this idea, saying that it is diversity in our ways of living and thinking that leads to human happiness.

Even so, Mill wants to keep an idea of progressive improvement of ways of life that seems to imply a hierarchy among human preferences and practices—that is, he believes that some choices are better than others, and these will drive progress.

Overlooked

A central strand of *On Liberty* is the influence of Romantic* artists and poets and of utopian socialist* individualism. This influence is detectable in Mill's account of the progressive character of individual fulfillment.

The consensus view of *On Liberty* as a definitive statement of classical liberalism tends to understate this aspect of the text. But reinterpretations of Mill's thought, both by his contemporaries and by recent thinkers, have recovered this strand of individualism, to various ends.

One issue raised by those who have attempted to recover and interpret the Romantic, perfectionist aspect of Mill's individualism is the question of Mill's elitism.

Thinkers such as the British historian Maurice Cowling and the conservative political theorist Shirley Letwin[1] have argued that *On Liberty*'s emphasis on innovative and outstanding characters amounts to a hierarchy of tastes, opinions, and preferences. According to this interpretation, the most cultivated and intellectually independent people challenge the mediocrity of established traditions.

As the British philosopher John Skorupski notes: "What often raises readers' hackles here is Mill's elitism: he thinks that only some people are competent to judge the quality, as against the quantity, of pleasure."[2] This elitism leads to a fundamentally illiberal strand in Mill's thought; his desire, it seems, is to reduce "diversity" to an instrument for protecting outstanding individuals from the mediocre masses.

An alternative analysis by twentieth-century thinkers such as the Indian American economic theorist Amartya Sen* and the American political philosopher Martha Nussbaum* draws on Mill's version of personal fulfillment to defend state assistance for families, the poor, and the unemployed.[3]

These scholars refuse to accept *On Liberty* as illiberal, seeing Mill's description of individuality as an ideal for everyone. Basic needs such as education and money to live on must be met before people are free to develop their tastes and opinions and try out different ways of life. They also highlight Mill's use of individual creativity to defend the value of culture as a social good that should be protected by the state.

Mill's rejection of the legacy of the radical* Protestant Christian movement known as the Puritans* is often overlooked, too. He was in favor of the arts; the Puritans considered them to be a hedonistic pursuit and a waste of energy better used on pious living. Modern scholars are looking again at Mill's doctrine of the Art of Life* (action in pursuit of desirable things) spelled out in *A System of Logic* (1843) to recover this side of his work. This could change the modern view of his work as being all about negative liberty (limiting state power over people), which neglects his celebration of individuals flourishing away from state influence.

NOTES

1   See Maurice Cowling's *Mill and Liberalism* (1963) and Shirley Letwin's *The Pursuit of Certainty* (1965). American historian Gertrude Himmelfarb attributes this elitist strand to *On Liberty*, in particular, and views it as one portion of a broad shift in Mill's thought after his wife's death. See Gertrude Himmelfarb, introduction to *Essays in Politics and Culture*, by John Stuart Mill (New York: Doubleday and Co., 1963).

2   John Skorupski, *Why Read Mill Today?* (London: Routledge, 2006), 33.

3   Amartya Sen, "A Decade of Human Development," *Journal of Human Development* 1.1 (2000): 17–23.

MODULE 7
ACHIEVEMENT

KEY POINTS

- John Stuart Mill takes classical utilitarian* theory and introduces new considerations, showing how this new understanding can keep government at a proper distance from individual life and thought.

- *On Liberty* spoke directly to the drastic political and social transformations taking place throughout Western Europe during the eighteenth and nineteenth centuries.

- The text can be seen as having less relevance in societies that place greater emphasis on collective identity than individual pursuits.

Assessing the Argument

On Liberty is clearly the work of a mature thinker. John Stuart Mill offers a new approach to the principle of utility* (right action leads to more happiness and wrong action to less), based on the work of older philosophical radicals.* These included his own father, the philosopher James Mill,* and the founder of utilitarian theory, Jeremy Bentham,* both of whom educated the author in their school of thought.

Mill moves utilitarian thinking on by questioning the philosophical framework and the vision of society it defends. He uses *On Liberty* to set out his philosophical and political position in the light of new influences on his adult thinking, such as the English Romantic movement* and the Saint-Simonian* school's[1] utopian philosophies of progress, industry, and socialism.

He weaves the insights he takes from these approaches into classical utilitarian thinking. Mill uses his expanded theory to discuss the

> ❝ Mill's approach followed the achievement of many constitutional, economic, and administrative reforms during the 1830s and 40s. These were reforms that he approved, including some that Benthamites had proposed. The Reform Act was passed in 1832 and the Poor Law Amendment Act in 1834. Public pressure for free trade developed during the 1830s and led to the abolition of the corn laws in 1846. Of course, Mill was not equally pleased by all the changes that had been made, but he witnessed large steps towards improvements in both institutions and policies. ❞
>
> Joseph Hamburger, "Individuality and Moral Reform: the Rhetoric of Liberty and the Reality of Restraint in Mill's *On Liberty*"

implications for politics and the need to protect the freedom to speak and live as we choose.

By and large, he is successful in achieving these aims in *On Liberty*. The final treatise tackles the problem of the tyranny of the majority on the progress of knowledge, and sets out exactly how important individuality is to human well-being.

Mill puts his theory to work by exploring its practical impact on how society is governed. The core argument of *On Liberty* flows from its opening question—how much power should society and the state have over each person? He attempts to clarify the forms of this power and—crucially—the threat it poses to personal freedom.

Achievement in Context

On Liberty was published at a time of great social upheaval. Mill made a clarion call for a rapidly changing world to value freedom and reject government interference in private life.

He waded into debates over the proper character and power of modern government amid enormous transformations in England. Rapid development of industrial production and ambitious building programs to improve communications and trade links saw the rise of a class-based, city-dwelling, "commercial society" across Western Europe.

These social changes brought political changes with them, speeding up the shift to representative government and increased democratic accountability. More people were involved in politics, both through the work of the British political parties and thanks to an active print media that gave public opinion a voice. In *On Liberty*, Mill observes the notable effect that these changes were beginning to have on the quality of public debate, and accurately[2] predicts that, in the future, commercial society would have a worrying impact on the life of every individual.

The global march of liberal* democratic institutions and ideals from the nineteenth century worked to reproduce some of the social and political conditions that Mill grapples with in *On Liberty*. The influence of Western political and economic systems in shaping non-Western societies is a point of great intellectual debate. However, the history of colonial and postcolonial international development shows that many parts of the world adopted systems based on state protection of civil and political rights. These included private property, private contract, free speech, elective representation, and the right to collective action.

Many historians have questioned this kind of center-out model, suggesting instead that liberal thought developed with input from around the world as experiences on the "periphery" were often transferred back to the "center" (a good example is Mill's concern with the abolition of slavery in the United States). Even so, *On Liberty*'s relevance was felt in political and academic circles reaching far beyond Western Europe.

Limitations

It is difficult to overstate the impact that Mill's ideas have had on Western political thought in the nineteenth, twentieth, and twenty-first centuries. *On Liberty* is central to liberal understanding and has proved relevant to different cultures and political traditions around the world. The key question Mill raises about the proper role of the state still has to be answered by all democracies.

Societies with traditions of understanding and organizing politics around collective identity and interests, however, have found Mill's ideas less relevant. Modern scholars point to China, Islamic states, and traditional societies across the globe, which see translating collective-based values and practices into Mill's liberal model of individual rights as a challenge.

Many societies value the collective will more highly than that of the individual. When such collective identities and state institutions include a theocratic* system (that is, a system in which the lines between state governance and religion are blurred), they can clash with Mill's view of religion as a private matter. In these cases, the value of individual rights to think or behave differently is weighed against the value of enforcing shared belief systems and cultural practices.

NOTES

1   Alan Ryan, *J. S. Mill* (London and Boston: Routledge and Kegan Paul, 1974).

2   See Toshihiko Iwama, "Parties, Middle-Class Voters, and the Urban Community: Rethinking the Halifax Parliamentary Borough Elections, 1832–1852," *Northern History* 51.1(2014): 91–112.

MODULE 8
PLACE IN THE AUTHOR'S WORK

KEY POINTS

- John Stuart Mill's books had an academic impact in several areas, earning the position of standard texts in the fields of logic, political economy,* and political and moral philosophy.

- *On Liberty* came in the middle of Mill's career, linking his earlier systematic work on utilitarianism* to his later defense of political liberalism.*

- The text was influential in Mill's lifetime and went on to become his most famous book in the centuries that followed.

Positioning

John Stuart Mill was a leading figure in the English intellectual life of the mid-nineteenth century and *On Liberty* was not the only one of his books to have an impact on philosophical discussion among politicians and scholars. His works made a significant contribution to the fields of political economy,[1] political and moral philosophy, and the study of logic.

During his early career, Mill established his academic reputation with *A System of Logic* (1843); this became the standard work on logic during the nineteenth century. His ideas on the philosophy of science remained the most decisive treatment of the subject for half a century after its publication. *Principles of Political Economy* (1848) was the definitive text of classical liberal economics* of the day.

Mill's later work also deserves attention. *Utilitarianism* (1861) and *The Subjection of Women* (1869) continue the themes of *On Liberty*. The

❝ That the principle which regulates the existing social relations between the two sexes—the legal subordination of one sex to the other—is wrong itself, and now one of the chief hindrances to human improvement; and that it ought to be replaced by a principle of perfect equality, admitting no power or privilege on the one side, nor disability on the other. **❞**

John Stuart Mill, The Subjection of Women

Subjection of Women, which Mill wrote with the assistance of his stepdaughter, the early feminist Helen Taylor,* states the social value of granting equal rights to women. *Utilitarianism* continues Mill's mission to correct and clarify the orthodox utilitarian theory of society. Both essays stand as important statements of moral and political philosophy in their own right. *Utilitarianism* and *On Liberty* are Mill's most enduring works.

Integration

Utilitarianism and *On Liberty* share certain key concerns; both rely on the utilitarian philosophy Mill set out in *A System Of Logic.*

"Utility"* refers to judging an action by whether it promotes the greatest happiness—a calculation that guides practical reasoning. Although this is largely taken from Jeremy Bentham,* Mill makes crucial additions to the idea through a discussion of the moral status of the principle of utility.[2] His moral argument rests on the essential value of individuality in promoting the greatest human happiness—an idea that only comes properly into focus when he departs from the austere utilitarianism of his father's generation.

It is possible to trace the development of Mill's thought through the way he molds utilitarianism to fit his ideas. He explores the positive and progressive value of individualism, challenging the negative view of increasing happiness through the avoidance of pain. He takes the exploration to a conclusion in *On Liberty*, settling on the best way to achieve general happiness: the promotion of free intellectual and cultural development.

Mill's unique brand of liberalism can be seen in later works such as *The Subjection of Women*, in which he argues that educating and empowering women advances human freedom: "The legal subordination of one sex to the other … is wrong itself, and now one of the chief hindrances to human improvement."[3] The political theorist Martha Nussbaum describes Mill as "a genuine ally of women's equality"—something "so rare in the history of philosophy."[4]

According to the philosopher John Skorupski, Mill's work shares "a very strong unifying theme: it is his lifelong effort to weave together the insights of the Enlightenment in which he had been reared, and the nineteenth-century reaction against it, a reaction sometimes romantic, sometimes historical and conservative, and often both."[5]

Significance

On Liberty has not lost its influence in the century and a half since it was published.

The defense of individual freedom through the "harm principle"* is still used by political thinkers trying to agree on the amount of power the state should be allowed over the individual. *On Liberty* is a classic text for all students of politics, moral philosophy, and social theory. The book was widely known during Mill's lifetime and now stands as his most famous work.

The text's continuing relevance for scholarly and popular debates is in little doubt. The ideas Mill shares in *On Liberty* are central to the political and economic values of liberal democracy. Mill's theories can, however, be employed by many political camps; the theory of individualism alone is so expansive that it can be incorporated in both right-wing libertarian* politics (opposed to the state as a political body) and to progressive welfare policy (which assumes that the state can play a useful role in protecting the well-being of its citizens).

Politicians, social theorists, and economists invoke Mill in the defense of policies that are largely opposed to one another. This is sometimes through different readings of Mill's limits on state power in protecting shared goods and promoting shared values through welfare, education, health insurance, and public investment in natural and cultural resources.

NOTES

1   See, for example, Stephen Nathanson, "John Stuart Mill on Economic Justice and the Alleviation of Poverty," *Journal of Social Philosophy* 43.2 (2012): 161–76.

2   John Stuart Mill, *On Liberty and Other Essays* (Oxford: Oxford University Press, 1998), VIII–XV.

3   John Stuart Mill, *The Subjection of Women* (Paris: Editions Artisan Devereaux, 2014), 7.

4   Christine Smallwood, "Back Talk: Martha C. Nussbaum," *The Nation* (2010), http://www.thenation.com/article/back-talk-martha-c-nussbaum# Accessed 10 May 2015.

5   John Skorupski, *Why Read Mill Today?* (London: Routledge, 2006), 4.

SECTION 3
IMPACT

THE FIRST RESPONSES

KEY POINTS

- James Fitzjames Stephen,* one of the first critics of *On Liberty*, argued that social progress requires more state interference than Mill's "harm principle"* allows.

- After the work's publication, Mill's intellectual development and political activity show that critics of his book did not prompt him into changing his position.

- Mill continued to argue for radical* politics in his writing well after *On Liberty*.

Criticism

Among the early responses to John Stuart Mill's *On Liberty* was James Fitzjames Stephen's 1872 *Liberty, Equality, Fraternity*.[1] In it, Stephen criticized the "harm principle"—Mill's rule for stopping a person from doing something only if their action would harm somebody else—for limiting state intervention.

Stephen said Mill's principle of utility* actually justifies the wide use of state action to promote utility (that is, the outcome society wants). Mill's text, Stephen went on, denied the historical evidence that social progress requires some use of moral, social, legal, and religious sanctions. Social progress, he argued, needs more state interference than Mill's own rules would allow.

Another notable critic of Mill was his fellow British philosopher Matthew Arnold;* although Arnold was an outspoken critic of utilitarianism,* he did share some major points of agreement with Mill on topical issues such as education. By contrast, the British biologist Thomas Henry Huxley* accused Mill of being against state

> ❝ Christian morality (so called) has all the characters of a reaction; it is, in great part, a protest against Paganism. Its ideal is negative rather than positive; passive rather than action; innocence rather than Nobleness; Abstinence from Evil, rather than energetic Pursuit of Good: in its precepts (as has been well said) 'thou shalt not' predominates unduly over 'thou shalt.' ❞
>
> John Stuart Mill, *On Liberty*

intervention in education. Huxley wanted taxes to pay for popular education and, suggesting that Mill rejected this idea, charged him with setting the bar too high for intervention in support of common goals.[2]

Finally, the utilitarian philosopher Henry Sidgwick* attacked Mill's version of moral utilitarianism, arguing that his view of human nature does not allow for "social facts" that affect the outcome. For him, Mill did not take into account historical factors that complicate the relationship between the pleasure of an act and its moral utility in contributing to the greatest happiness.

Responses

Mill's account of the rights of the individual in both *On Liberty* and later essays came under attack from mainstream politicians and more philosophically minded intellectuals. His views on equal rights for women and ex-slaves were certainly radical for the time; the Scottish philosopher Thomas Carlyle* went as far as to describe Mill's support for such controversial issues as a compromise of philosophical integrity.

Early criticisms of *On Liberty* fell into three categories. First, there were those who disliked the political radicalism of Mill's defense of individual liberty against state power and social opinion. Second, some thinkers took issue with Mill over utilitarianism as a social theory. And third, Mill was accused of elitism in his individualist view of society where the cultured lead the way to superior lifestyles and ideas.

Mill did not change his views when *On Liberty* came under fire. Instead he remained a political radical to the end of his life. He continued to publish political essays, debate with his contemporaries and take part in politics as a member of Parliament. There he spoke out on behalf of radical causes such as women's rights, racial equality, and religious freedom. So despite various critical responses when *On Liberty* appeared in 1859, Mill stood by his core arguments.

Conflict and Consensus

The issue of religious freedom Mill raised in *On Liberty* became a central concern of his writing in later years. *On Liberty* was seen by some as anti-Christian for its attack on the role of religious dogma in stifling individual thought. It was seen as a defense of the artistic, pleasure-seeking side of self-fulfillment against the English Puritan* disapproval of sensual interests. Mill warmed to his theme again in the essay "The Utility of Religion" (1874).[3]

Mill's *Autobiography* (1874) gives us his own account of how his opinions changed throughout his life. In the final pages he laments how the middle classes settle for traditional beliefs without ever questioning them. He admits that experience taught him that the intellectual and moral improvement of the middle classes and "uncultivated masses" requires a radical education capable of bringing about a change in "the fundamental constitutions in their modes of thought," such that new opinions could see the light of day.[4] He complains about the suffocating effect of "the old opinions in religion, morals, and politics," which, despite having been largely discredited, still show "vitality enough left to be an effectual obstacle to the rising up of better opinions on the same subjects."[5]

NOTES

1   James Fitzjames Stephen, *Liberty, Equality, Fraternity and Three Brief Essays* (Chicago: Chicago University Press, 1992).

2   Maurice Mandelbaum, *History, Man, and Reason: A Study in Nineteenth-Century Thought* (Baltimore: John Hopkins Press, 1971), 458 n88.

3   See John Stuart Mill, "The Utility of Religion" in *Three Essays on Religion: Nature, The Utility of Religion, Theism* (Amherst, NY: Prometheus Books, 1998).

4   John Stuart Mill, *An Early Draft of John Stuart Mill's Autobiography* (Urbana: University of Illinois Press, 1961), 176.

5   Mill, *Early Draft*, 177; Joseph Hamburger, *John Stuart Mill On Liberty and Control* (Princeton: Princeton University Press, 1999).

THE EVOLVING DEBATE

KEY POINTS

- John Stuart Mill's definition of civil liberty* and his "harm principle"* to control state interference are the starting point for understanding the evolution of liberal* thought.

- The renewed interest in classical liberal principles since the 1970s has seen *On Liberty* put to a variety of opposing uses by different scholars, from criticism of welfare-state measures to calls for more state intervention to help the needy.

- *On Liberty* still has a role in modern democratic theory, especially its warnings about potential tension between popular participation and the quality of popular tastes and opinions.

Uses and Problems

Although John Stuart Mill's definition of civil liberty—defended by the "harm principle" for keeping the state at bay—has become an integral part of liberal thought, the ideas offered in *On Liberty* create dilemmas for modern thinkers who want to apply Mill's rules for guaranteeing freedom to society today.

Liberal theorists writing after Mill, such as the politician Leonard Trelawny Hobhouse* and the economist John Atkinson Hobson,* tried to resolve some of the difficulties of Mill's text. They insist there is more to individual liberty than negative rights to be left alone by the state; to enjoy individual freedom a person needs to have their basic needs—education, employment, the right to vote, and welfare insurance, for example—met. So these social progressives use the idea of positive rights to describe necessary state intervention that provides people with essentials.

> ❝ The likings and dislikings of society, or of some powerful portion of it, are thus the main thing which has practically determined the rules laid down for general observance, under the penalties of law or opinion. And in general, those who have been in advance of society in thought and feeling, have left this condition of things unassailed in principle, however they may have come into conflict with it in some of its details. ❞
>
> John Stuart Mill, *On Liberty*

Recent decades have seen political attempts to reconcile individuality with other values such as religious or cultural practices; this can lead to a tension between the need for individual rights and the need for collective rights.

Later twentieth-century political thinkers such as the American philosopher John Rawls* and the German philosopher Thomas Pogge* have translated socialist-progressive language into the language of social justice;* social-justice liberalism attempts to develop a new theoretical framework to weigh the benefit of state protection for some against the harms of state intervention for all.

Schools of Thought

The renewed interest in classical liberal principles that emerged in the final decades of the twentieth century drew heavily on Mill's ideas. Laissez-faire* principles (roughly, the argument that state intervention in the economy or in the life of the citizen is undesirable) resurfaced in the twentieth century in the work of the influential economists Milton Friedman,* Friedrich Hayek,* and Robert Nozick.*

Neoliberals* and neoconservatives,* who emphasize the supposed desirability of free-market competition, argue that welfare-state policies such as income support, public health care, increased public education, and childcare are examples of the state overreaching by being too involved in the citizen's private life. These thinkers adapt classical liberal principles associated with Mill to advance free-market capitalism and the break up of the consensus around the welfare state.

A competing school of liberal theory includes thinkers such as John Rawls, Amartya Sen,* and Michael Sandel.* These political theorists attempt to balance the value of liberty with the values of justice and equality, relating to Mill's understanding of the need to balance moral duties to family and society with the individual's right to non-interference; they use Mill's ideas on progress to explore collective agreements over shared goods such as economic resources, scientific-technical research and industry, communications and transportation, cultural goods, and education. Although their emphasis on justice and equality moves past Mill's arguments for thinking about social obligations, it is arguably in harmony with his concerns.

In Current Scholarship

On Liberty is still providing food for liberal thought as modern scholars wrestle with the complex challenges of modern society. In the nineteenth century Mill accurately predicted a future in which we would experience a strain between the value of increased democratic accountability on one hand, and concerns over the "mediocre" quality of popular opinions and tastes on the other. Mill raises the possibility of having to temper the force of popular opinion by looking for guidance from "a more highly gifted and instructed One or Few."[1]

A key concern in current political debate is the quality of democratic participation when political engagement is reduced to the casting of a vote every few years, and with the emergence of a mass media that effectively reproduces majority opinions and prejudices. Democratic theorists tend to celebrate increased participation in government and more accountability. Conservative scholars, however, referring to Mill's worries about the power of a stifling, mediocre middle class over democratic institutions, are sympathetic to Mill's ideal of government run by a cultivated elite of experts.

Mill's arguments in *On Liberty* are still used to test the models of social behavior used in economics and the social sciences. They are made more effective by adding the restrictions on individual choice Mill identified. Sen, for example, draws on Mill's theory of the force of popular opinion to argue that people do not act independently in their private lives, being influenced by the actions of others.

A new literature has emerged exploring Mill's vision of individual fulfillment and his theory of the Art of Life* (outlined in 1843 in his *A System of Logic*), which was inspired by Aristotle.*[2] This is in direct response to what some scholars argue is an insufficiently detailed understanding of the individual in neoliberal theory, especially in economics.

Finally, contemporary thinkers are seeking to recover the active and holistic (that is, integrated and universal) account of individual fulfillment they find in *On Liberty*.

NOTES

1   "No government by a democracy or a numerous aristocracy, either in its political acts or in the opinions, qualities, and tone of mind which it fosters, ever did or could rise above mediocrity, except in so far as the sovereign Many have let themselves be guided (which in the best times they have always done) by the counsels and influence of a more highly gifted and instructed One or Few." John Stuart Mill, *On Liberty* (New York: Dover Publications, 2002), 55.

2   Mill describes the inextricable link between a person's opinions and understandings and his or her life experiences; and he defends experimentation in new forms of life on these grounds. Individuality in this holistic sense resembles Aristotle's philosophy of *Eudaimonia*, which saw the achievement of wisdom, virtue, and happiness as linked to a set of life practices and habits that promote individual flourishing.

IMPACT AND INFLUENCE TODAY

KEY POINTS

- *On Liberty* has taken its place among the most distinguished and respected texts in Western political and social thought.

- Mill's theories about democracy, social progress, and the balance between individual liberty and social duty fueled a debate on the nature of freedom that continues to this day.

- Thinkers such as Friedrich Hayek* and John Rawls* have responded to the challenges offered by Mill's particular version of liberalism.*

Position

Since the death of John Stuart Mill in 1873, *On Liberty* has come to be regarded as one of the most important works in Western thought. For the generations of scholars that came after him, Mill's book has been a definitive statement of the liberal understanding of the world.

The work's influence extends beyond philosophical circles to a wider audience of statesmen and policy makers. Different political and philosophical camps have claimed Mill's theories for their own ends, using them in defense of a variety of political positions. Tensions in Mill's own view of the prospects for democracy, the role of elite culture in shaping social progress, and the proper balance between individual freedom and social duties opened the door to a debate spanning three centuries.

Mill's subtle and persuasive argument for the social value of individuality makes *On Liberty* the voice of a crucial period in modern political thought. Mill's enduring essay stands at the crossroads of two

> 66 The beliefs which we have the most warrant for have
> no safeguard, but a standing invitation to the whole
> world to prove them unfounded. 99
>
> John Stuart Mill, *On Liberty*

eras. Behind him is old classical liberalism, struggling to draw a line between private life and the authorities. In front, an era of representative government and middle-class economic and political power with its new political flashpoints.

Mill was part of an intellectual world in which the interventionist policies of socialists such as Robert Owen* or the followers of the Saint-Simonian* school clashed with laissez-faire*—non-interference—policies of orthodox liberals such as Mill's father, James Mill,* and the philosopher John Locke.* Between these extremes Mill carved a progressive liberal path. He recognized the potential for state institutions to be tools for social improvement, while seeking to limit their ability to impose beliefs or ways of life.

Interaction

Following World War II and the onset of the Cold War* (a period of economic and political hostility between the communist* USSR* and the West) liberal principles had a new lease of life. Faced with a polarized world, liberals advanced new takes on classic values such as brakes on state power, a hands-off policy over private activities and the value of individualism in human progress.

Although these shared some of Mill's core values, prominent neoliberal* thinkers—advocates for an unhindered free market—such as Friedrich Hayek positioned themselves against Mill's brand of liberalism. Setting himself apart from Mill, Hayek saw liberalism as fundamentally a theory of society rather than of nature. For him, this was a recognition of the spontaneous order that emerges from social complexity without the intervention of central planning. Hayek's defense of the progressive force of individualism clearly owes something to *On Liberty.*

New challenges to Mill included the American philosopher John Rawls's influential *A Theory of Justice* (1971). Rawls declares that the first principle of a just society is to maximize the amount of liberty everyone enjoys equally. With its limits on state intervention to prevent harm, *On Liberty*'s version of individual freedom does not support Rawls's principle.

Social justice* means taking steps to ensure equality—but that is ruled out by the utilitarian* defense of liberty. Rawls reopens the debate over liberalism and social justice in politics. A major voice in this debate is the rational-choice school of social theory, which borrows from economics game theory* to work out efficient social policy.[1] Modern economics translates the utility* calculation, based on the rational judgment of whether an action adds to happiness, into a logic of choice using a series of numbered preferences.

Rational-choice theories are alternative ways of judging whether state or society ought to intervene—by weighing the benefits to some people against the losses for others.

The Continuing Debate

It is interesting to note that these challenges to *On Liberty* often draw on theories that did not exist during Mill's lifetime in order to defend his liberal doctrine. Hayek, for example, uses innovations in theories of knowledge to defend the laissez-faire approach to social complexity. Rational-choice theorists integrate advances in statistical modeling to predict the behavior of individuals and argue that people tend to maximize their desired outcomes.

The use of these new methods is a source of great intellectual debate in the field of political theory and the social sciences.

Defenders of the social-justice approach, such as Rawls and the political theorist Michael Sandel,* challenge *On Liberty*'s emphasis on non-interference by the state. Though holding very different views on some issues, these authors agree that classical liberalism does not pay enough attention to collective goals such as equality of opportunity and minimum standards of employment and education.

To answer these criticisms, liberal thinkers such as Amartya Sen* and Martha Nussbaum* highlight Mill's account of the diversity of human preferences and ways of life. They argue that this diversity is so profound that it prevents enough people agreeing on collective goals, so it is not worth the infringement on liberty.

NOTES

1   Exemplary works include Gary Becker's *Economic Approach to Human Behavior* (1976) and Milton Friedman's "The Methodology of Positive Economics" (1953).

WHERE NEXT?

KEY POINTS

- John Stuart Mill's *On Liberty* will remain on the essential reading list for scholars and politicians because its ideas are central to the moral, political, and economic values of liberal* democracy.

- Mill has many disciples who use his ideas in modern discourse in very different ways, from neoliberals* and neoconservatives,* who favor the aggressive promotion of free-market economics, to social-justice* liberals, who argue for the state meeting basic human needs.

- Ultimately, *On Liberty* is a seminal text because of Mill's powerful and unprecedented defense of individual freedom as inseparable from social progress.

Potential

The power of John Stuart Mill's *On Liberty* remains undimmed. Scholars continue to reach for the text in order to understand the principles and problems at the heart of liberal democracy. Societies that organize themselves in this way owe a huge debt to Mill. He sets out the rules and values of a system followed by nations around the world. As the scholar Andrew Norton notes: "Like other great political book*s, On Liberty* remains worth reading because it asks questions that still need answers."[1]

Mill's "liberal bible" is still the subject of a fair amount of controversy, however.[2] The work has elements that can be seen as contradicting each other. These include Mill's defense of a "hands-off" approach to keeping private life private, an idea that defines classical liberalism, and his belief in socialist ideals of collective economic control.

> **"**A person may cause evil to others not only by his actions but by his inaction, and in either case he is justly accountable to them for the injury. **"**
>
> John Stuart Mill, *On Liberty*

Such puzzles keep *On Liberty* relevant to every age: "Despite its apparent absoluteness, *On Liberty* refuses to fade away partly because its contradictions and confusions are much like our own. Is freedom really an end in itself, or a means to something else? What obligations does each individual have to all the other individuals who together make up society?"[3]

Different readings of Mill show up today when *On Liberty* is invoked in support of contrary policies. Mill can be seen as backing an active role for government in moving society forward through progressive education and social policies.

An alternative view of Mill's liberalism could support contemporary neoconservatives* and libertarians* in their call to protect the pursuits of the free individual from government interference. Regardless, it is clear that Mill's ideas are relevant to many of our era's most perplexing political scenarios. These include whether legitimate central authority can be created in the countries that experienced political uprisings in the Arab Spring*—including Tunisia, Egypt, Libya, and Yemen—to whether China's one-party system of control can endure.[4]

Future Directions

Modern disciples of Mill can be divided broadly into four camps: neoliberals, social-justice liberals, contemporary classical liberals, and critics who deplore the impact of popular opinion and mass culture on the quality of public debate and democratic government.

Much of the split can be traced to the 1970s, when classical liberal thought was brought back into the academic spotlight by the philosopher John Rawls's* *A Theory of Justice* (1971). This book prompted fresh debate around liberal social-justice theories—with thinkers on both sides of the divide claiming *On Liberty* for their cause.

On the social-justice side, Rawls criticizes the principles of non-interventionist laissez-faire* economics for failing to take account of the social conditions that shape a person's ability to practice their rights and liberties. The political theorist Martha Nussbaum* and the economist Amartya Sen* point to Mill's radical* position as a champion of equal rights and opportunity and call for economic theory to reflect the needs of women and the economically disadvantaged; for them, this involves removing the social barriers that prevent people from exercising the right to freedom of enterprise and freedom of conscience that Mill advocated.[5]

On the laissez-faire liberalism side are thinkers such as Friedrich Hayek,* Milton Friedman,* and Robert Nozick.* They say that people flourish when their individual pursuits and beliefs are protected from state intervention. The emphasis on private affairs as a realm of individual freedom and innovation is taken from Mill's defense of individuality. They argue that social order is best maintained by allowing free-market forces to coordinate people's behavior.

The theory of social order by way of market forces is not, however, the basis of Mill's defense of the "harm principle."* *On Liberty* defends the principle in the interest of protecting liberty, and Mill's comments on laissez-faire economic principles are based on his belief that the private sphere tends to manage economics better than the government.

Contemporary laissez-faire liberals could be understood as using a theory of society that is absent from *On Liberty*.

Summary

Mill devoted his life to the defense of individual freedom as an essential component of social progress. *On Liberty* is where he sets out his best arguments for gradually improving society—and therefore human wisdom and happiness—through liberal institutions such as a public education system, representative government, and a capitalist market economy.

Aside from Mill's powerful arguments, the subject matter of *On Liberty* has ensured it has never fallen into obscurity. It is a core text for one of the dominant political doctrines of our day—liberal democracy. Freedom of speech and religion and the right to private pursuits are the foundational values of the modern liberal state. And *On Liberty* is part of the cultural and intellectual heritage that built these civil liberties into the liberal conscience.

Modern scholars and political thinkers turn to *On Liberty* not only to understand the history of Western thought but also to tackle pressing modern problems. Accordingly, Mill's "harm principle" has been used to criticize state practices such as anti-drug laws and whether the government has the right to enforce laws against suicide. In the legal world, Mill's ideas help to draft legislation and articulate legal precedent for what counts as acceptable language.

As one journalist has put it:"Mill's ideas are everywhere. Appeal to them was made frequently in the debate over the permissibility of publishing cartoons offensive to Islam and to the jailing in Austria of Holocaust denier David Irving. … Recent discussions of happiness and the difficulty inherent in its pursuit cannot avoid appealing to his authority."[6]

In both the philosophical realm and real-world politics, *On Liberty* has lost none of its appeal.

NOTES

1   Andrew Norton, "*On Liberty* at 150," *Policy* 25.2 (2009), 52.

2   See Joseph Hamburger, *John Stuart Mill On Liberty and Control* (Princeton: Princeton University Press, 1999).

3   Christopher Clausen, "John Stuart Mill's 'Very Simple Principle,'" *The Wilson Quarterly* 33.2 (2009), 46.

4   Robert D. Kaplan, "John Stuart Mill, Dead Thinker of the Year," *Foreign Policy* 190 (2011), 94.

5   Christine Smallwood, "Back Talk: Martha C. Nussbaum," *The Nation* (2010), http://www.thenation.com/article/back-talk-martha-c-nussbaum# Accessed 10 May 2015.

6   Anthony Skelton, "Liberty's godfather," *The Globe and Mail*, May 20, 2006.

GLOSSARY

GLOSSARY OF TERMS

American Revolution (1765–83): also referred to as the "American War of Independence," the American Revolution was the rejection of British rule over the 13 American colonies, the rebellion that ensued, and the subsequent establishment of the United States.

Arab Spring: a series of protests, demonstrations, riots, revolutions, and civil wars that began in 2010 in Tunisia and quickly spread through a large segment of the Arab world.

Art of Life: Mill's name for his theory of practical reason. He divides the Art of Life into three "departments": Morality (the right), Prudence or Policy (the expedient), and Aesthetics (the beautiful or noble).

Atheist: a person who does not believe in the existence of a "supreme being" or god.

Canonical: part of a tradition of great works of history, literature or intellectual theory.

Church of England: the state Church in England, with the monarch as its head. A Christian Church that combines Roman Catholic and Protestant traditions, it traces its Anglican identity to the Reformation in the sixteenth century.

Civil liberty: the limit to how far a society can exercise power over an individual. Mill defines three aspects of individual liberty: inner conscience and belief; tastes and pursuits; and action in concert with others. The harm principle stipulates that these forms of individual liberty are to be protected from intervention by the state or social coercion except when they cause harm to another individual's interest.

Classical economics: a school of economic thought associated with British theorists from the late eighteenth and early nineteenth centuries, among them Adam Smith* and John Stuart Mill. It focuses on economic growth and the belief that markets should be unregulated.

Classical liberal economics: based on the principle of individual economic freedom, as defined by the concept of individual private property and freedom of contract. It describes the market as a self-regulating mechanism that provides a sphere of autonomous, private pursuits outside of the state.

The Cold War: military tension between the United States of America and the USSR* and their respective allies that developed after World War II. The Cold War lasted from around 1945 to 1991.

Communism: an ideology and movement based on fostering human equality through the elimination of private property and market forces. Various forms of communism have been attempted by states such as the USSR,* China, and Cuba.

East India Company: English company established in 1600 to trade with the Far East and India; it took a political role and became an instrument of British imperialism, with its own armies, in the eighteenth and nineteenth centuries. As a result of the Indian Mutiny (a revolt among Company troops in 1857–59) the British government took over the company, which was wound up in 1873.

The Enlightenment: a period of rapid cultural and intellectual development centered in Europe, lasting from the mid-seventeenth century through to the eighteenth century. Enlightenment thought inspired revolutionary social and political change by discrediting claims to authority based in medieval religion and social order.

French Revolution (1789–99): a period of social and political upheaval and reform. It resulted in the collapse of the monarchy and the aristocracy, helped to usher in modernity, and inspired the development of republican and democratic systems of government.

Game theory: used in many social sciences but principally in economics, this studies how groups of people interact. More specifically, it refers to the study of strategic decision-making, and has two main branches: cooperative and non-cooperative game theory.

Harm principle: a rule, proposed by Mill, that interference in individual liberty may only be justified in cases when an individual's actions will harm another's interests. It argues that when an individual's actions do *not* harm another individual, the state has no justification for intervening. If they do cause harm, the commonplace morality contained in law is brought to bear.

Historical materialism: an approach to the study of history, society, and economics according to which material forces (labor capacity and technology) are the chief influence on social and economic development.

Idealism: in philosophy, the idea that how we perceive objects determines their properties; objects do not possess properties in themselves.

The Industrial Revolution: the period of rapid industrial development from 1750 to 1840 that began in Great Britain and spread to North America, Western Europe, and Japan. The period was marked by increased industrial capacity to produce large quantities of goods for cheaper prices. These innovations led to increased trade in commodities and in raw goods and slaves.

Laissez-faire: in economics, this refers to a governmental policy of not intervening in the workings of the free market.

Legal positivist: a follower of legal philosopher John Austin who believes in positive law.

Liberalism: a political doctrine that centers on the protection of the individual and his or her freedom. It is associated with the philosophers John Locke and John Stuart Mill, the economist Adam Smith, and the statesman Thomas Jefferson. Liberalism aims to define the powers of government in terms of natural or God-given individual rights.

Libertarianism: a political philosophy that emphasizes the individual right to liberty. It can be understood as a form of liberalism.

Mechanism: a philosophical view that seeks to explain the social whole by analyzing the forces and actions of its parts—individual human beings. Psychology and sciences seeking to understand human nature could explain social phenomena by explaining the behavior of individuals, who acted in reciprocal relations to form the social whole.

Nationalist: a believer in loyalty to one's nation and perhaps in a national consciousness; often a supporter of national independence for one's country.

Neoconservatism: a branch of American conservatism that emphasizes the importance of free-market economics and the aggressive promotion of democracy by way of military force. Neoconservatives are also, generally speaking, neoliberals.

Neoliberalism: a political model that emphasizes free-market competition.

Organicism: the philosophical belief that the universe or society functions like a biological organism—that is, that all component parts are organic wholes. Organicism takes social institutions and relations as the unit of study in seeking to explain social phenomena. It emphasizes the impact of particular historical forms of thought and order on shaping human nature.

The Philosophical Radicals: Group of radical thinkers and authors, led by Jeremy Bentham and John Stuart Mill's father James Mill.

Political economy: a field of academic study that analyzes the influence of economic theory and methods on political ideology. As such, it commonly considers how different economic systems develop in various political institutions.

The Poor Laws: a system of poor relief from the fourteenth century to 1948 in England and Wales. The Old Poor Law was centered around the parish and tended to be implemented haphazardly and on a local level. The laws were reformed in 1834 and were centrally enforced, including widespread use of workhouses.

Positive law: in the context of John Austin's work, positive law means man-made rather than natural or moral laws.

Puritanism: a religious movement launched by sixteenth- and seventeenth-century English Protestants. Protestant reformists Martin Luther and John Calvin defined the new sect's renunciation of aesthetic ritualistic religious practice and stressed the individual responsibility for cultivating a godly life through religious scholarship, discipline, work, and sacrifice.

Radicalism: a term that refers to predominantly left-wing reform movements that aim to transform social structures. In the nineteenth century, philosophical radicals influenced by utilitarianism took a more moderate stance among radical reformers, and contributed to a successful drive for reform of the electoral system of Parliament.

The Reformation: the sixteenth-century Protestant movement led by Martin Luther and John Calvin that resulted in the founding of Lutheran and Reformed Christian churches that broke with the teachings of Roman Catholicism. In England, conflicts between Protestants and Catholics fuelled the English civil war of the seventeenth century.

Romanticism: a poetic movement of the late eighteenth and early nineteenth centuries that prized nature and the interior world of feeling. Among the most celebrated English Romantic poets were William Wordsworth and Samuel Taylor Coleridge.

Saint-Simonianism: the utopian socialist beliefs associated with French philosopher Claude Henri de Rouvroy, Comte de Saint-Simon. It centers on the scientific and industrial progress of man, made possible by the organization of finance and industry.

Scientific Revolution: the emergence of modern science. This period began in approximately 1550, lasted until the late eighteenth century, and was marked by influential developments in such fields as mathematics, physics, astronomy, biology, and chemistry.

Social contract: an agreement among the members of society to form a society and abide by its rules.

Social liberty: as defined by Mill himself, "social liberty" refers to "the nature and limits of the power which can be legitimately exercised by society over the individual."

Social justice: in its most general sense, this refers to a notion of equality or equal opportunity in society. In a theoretical sense, it refers to a perception of a productive democratic society that focuses on the welfare of citizens and is defined by collaborative efforts at local, national, and global level.

Theocracy: government by religious authorities. Today hybrid states that include religious and elected political authorities are also referred to as theocracies. Theocracies integrate religious teaching and doctrine into state legislation.

USSR (Union of Soviet Socialist Republics): a union of states that existed between 1922 and 1991. It contained numerous Soviet republics and was governed as a single-party state by the Communist Party, out of Moscow.

Utilitarianism: a philosophical school associated with the British philosophers Jeremy Bentham and James Mill. Utilitarianism uses the principle of utility as the basis for a calculation of moral and social goods. A good is defined by its degree of utility, according to which an action is right if it tends to promote happiness and wrong if it tends to produce the reverse of happiness.

Utility: John Stuart Mill's test for distinguishing between right actions (which promote human happiness) and wrong actions (which lead to unhappiness).

Utopian socialism: a movement associated with Claude Henri de Rouvroy, Comte de Saint-Simon and the Welsh social reformer Robert Owen inspired by utilitarian theory, often called utopian socialism for its utopian aspirations. Influential works include Owen's *A New View of Society* (1813) and Saint-Simon's *Nouveau Christianisme* (1825).

The Westminster Review: a British quarterly publication established by philosopher Jeremy Bentham in 1823 as an organ for the Philosophical Radicals and published for 90 years, 1824–1914. John Stuart Mill and his father, James, contributed several articles; Mary Ann Evans—better known as George Eliot, author of the novel *Middlemarch* (1871–2)— was assistant editor in 1850–4.

PEOPLE MENTIONED IN THE TEXT

Aristotle (384–322 B.C.E.) was an Ancient Greek philosopher and student of Plato. Along with the work of his teacher, Aristotle's work in physics, metaphysics, logic, rhetoric, aesthetics, politics and ethics, among other areas of study, defined the development of Western thought.

Matthew Arnold (1822–88) was an English cultural critic who advised the British government on education practices. He is best known for championing education as a tool of human progress. His influential works include *Democracy* (1879) and *Culture and Anarchy* (1867–68).

John Austin (1790–1859) was an English legal philosopher, whose contributions to the legal positivist approach were influenced by Jeremy Bentham's utilitarian philosophy.

Jeremy Bentham (1748–1832) was an English philosopher, social theorist, jurist, and one of the founders of utilitarian philosophy. Bentham applied tenets of utilitarian philosophy to develop proposals for social reform. His work was influential in the development of political economic thought, and liberal economic and political theory, including the work of John Stuart Mill.

Thomas Carlyle (1795–1881) was a Scottish philosopher and writer whose social criticism voiced the concerns of a rapidly changing society. *The French Revolution: A History* (1837) is among his most important works. He was also well known as an essayist.

Samuel Taylor Coleridge (1772–1834) was one of the preeminent thinkers of English Romanticism. His most famous poems were *The Rime of the Ancient Mariner* and *Kubla Khan*. The Romantic movement influenced both liberal and radical political thought of the day, as well as growing nationalist sentiment across Europe.

Auguste Comte (1798–1857) was a prominent French philosopher and founder of social theory. He attempted to tie social theory to positivist science for the purpose of providing a scientific groundwork to political reform. His influential works include *The Course in Positive Philosophy* (1830–42) and *A General View of Positivism* (1848).

Milton Friedman (1912–2006) was an influential American economist. His contributions to monetary theory provided a new defense of free-market economics that broke the consensus around the welfare-state economics of John Maynard Keynes. Friedman targeted *Capitalism and Freedom* (1962) at a popular audience. The book was a highly influential defense of free-market principles.

Friedrich Hayek (1899–1992) was born in Austria-Hungary and lived and worked in Great Britain. Hayek was a leading economist and philosopher of his day. His famous works including *The Road to Serfdom* (1944) and *The Constitution of Liberty* (1960) provided a renewed defense of classical liberal doctrine.

G. W. F. Hegel (1770–1831) was a German philosopher and major thinker of German Idealism, which challenged the practical philosophy of Immanuel Kant. Hegel introduced the dialectical philosophy of history that was widely influential in subsequent philosophies of society, including Marxist historical materialism.

Thomas Hobbes (1588–1679) was an English philosopher. He is seen as a founder of Western political theory and the tradition of social contract theory. *Leviathan, or the Matter, Forme, and Power of a Commonwealth, Ecclesiasticall and Civil* (1651) is his most influential work.

Leonard Trelawny Hobhouse (1864–1929) was an English liberal political theorist and sociologist, perhaps best known for his pioneering achievements in helping to establish and promote social liberalism.

John Atkinson Hobson (1858–1940) was an English economist and well-known critic of imperialism. He is best known for his "theory of consumption," which also served to discredit Hobson within the professional economics community.

Wilhelm von Humboldt (1767–1835) was a Prussian philosopher and civil servant. His essay *On the Limits of State Action* (published posthumously in 1850) was a major inspiration for *On Liberty*.

Thomas Henry Huxley (1825–95) was an English biologist and defender of the Darwinian theory of evolution. Huxley was a public intellectual who contributed to debates over the role of public education. In *Evolution and Ethics* Huxley argues that culture and education, in addition to biology, are responsible for the moral formation of human beings.

John Locke (1632–1704) was an English philosopher and leading thinker of the Enlightenment. His famous *Two Treatises of Government* (1689) and *A Letter Concerning Toleration* (1689) asserted what would become basic tenets of liberal theory.

T. B. Macaulay (1800–59) was an English politician and essayist. He wrote a famous critique of James Mill's utilitarianism in his 1829 essay "Mill on Government."

Thomas Malthus (1766–1834) was an English economist and demographer. He is best known for his theory on population growth, which spawned the school of thought known as Malthusianism.

James Mill (1773–1836) was a Scottish philosopher, political economist and founding thinker of British utilitarianism. His major works include *Elements of Political Economy*, published in 1821.

John Milton (1608–74) was a major English poet and prose writer, author of the epic poem *Paradise Lost* (1667) and pamphlets in which he called for the dissolution of the Church of England and supported the Puritan cause. His pamphlet *Aeropagitica* (1644) argued against restricting freedom of the press.

Andrew Norton (b. 1965) is an Australian researcher and program director of higher education at the Melbourne-based Grattan Institute. He writes extensively on higher education and classical liberalism.

Robert Nozick (1938–2002) was an American political philosopher and defender of libertarian values. His *Anarchy, State, and Utopia* (1974) gained recognition for its critique of John Rawls's defense of the role of the state in achieving a just society in his widely successful *A Theory of Justice* (1971).

Martha Nussbaum (b. 1947) is an American philosopher and political theorist known for her work expanding theories of justice to account for the conditions of women and the economically disadvantaged. Her *Frontiers of Justice: Disability, Nationality, Species*

Membership (2006) elaborated her theory of human capabilities as an addendum to John Rawls's theory of justice.

Robert Owen (1771–1858) was a Welsh political and social theorist, credited with articulating an early version of socialism, inspired by utilitarian theory, often called utopian socialism, for its utopian aspirations. Influential works include *A New View of Society Or, Essays on the Principle of the Formation of the Human Character, and the Application of the Principle to Practice* (1813).

Thomas Pogge (b. 1953) is a German philosopher based at Yale University, where he is director of the global justice program. His work focuses on moral and political philosophy, and he has written extensively on Immanuel Kant and John Rawls.

John Rawls (1921–2002) was an American philosopher often credited with reanimating Anglo-American political theory and moral philosophy in the 1970s with the publication of his influential *A Theory of Justice* (1971). Rawls developed an analytic style of addressing canonical questions of political theory.

David Ricardo (1772–1823) was an English political economist, considered one of the most influential classical economists. Ricardo is perhaps most famous for his development of the economic theory of comparative advantage.

Claude Henri de Rouvroy, Comte de Saint-Simon (1760–1825) was a French social reformer and philosopher, author of *Nouveau Christianisme* (1825). His followers developed a system of utopian socialist ideas known as Saint-Simonianism, which influenced Thomas Carlyle and John Stuart Mill.

Michael Sandel (b. 1953) is an American political philosopher. His critique of Rawls in *Liberalism and the Limits of Justice* (1982) charges that the demands of social justice cannot be met by assuming individuals can act as its interest-blind advocates.

Amartya Sen (b. 1933) is an influential economist and political philosopher. He was born in India and lives and works in the United States. His work on social choice theory, with its emphasis on collective goals that fall out of a narrowly economic calculus, has been influential in economics and social theory more broadly.

Henry Sidgwick (1838–1900) was an English utilitarian philosopher. He is best known for his contributions to utilitarian moral theory. *The Method of Ethics* (1874) is of continued relevance to the study of moral theory.

John Skorupski (b. 1946) is professor emeritus of modern philosophy at St Andrews University in Scotland. He is probably best known for his work on Mill, including the book *Why Read Mill Today?* (2006)

Adam Smith (1723–90) was a Scottish moral philosopher and political economist, who is arguably the father of modern economics. Smith is best known for his advancement of laissez-faire economic policies.

Socrates (470–399 B.C.E.) was a Greek philosopher, who profoundly influenced ancient and modern philosophy.

James Fitzjames Stephen (1829–94) was an English lawyer, high court judge and writer, who attacked the ideas in *On Liberty* in his own *Liberty, Equality, Fraternity* (1872). He argued for legal and state coercion. He wrote the book while traveling home from India, where he had served for three years in 1869–72 as a legal member on the Colonial Council.

Helen Taylor (1831–1907) was a British feminist, writer and actress. She was the daughter of Harriet Taylor Mill and stepdaughter of John Stuart Mill. After her mother's death in 1858 she collaborated with her stepfather for 15 years, promoting women's rights.

Harriet Taylor Mill (1807–58) was an English philosopher and women's rights advocate. While arguably most famous for her influence upon her second husband, John Stuart Mill, she was also a thinker in her own right and produced a substantial body of work.

Alexis de Tocqueville (1805–59) was a French political theorist and author of *Democracy in America* (1835, 1840), the famous work of political theory in which he elaborates the social bases of democratic government from an analysis of American society.

William Wordsworth (1770–1850) was an English poet whose *Lyrical Ballads* (1798), co-authored with Samuel Taylor Coleridge, is credited with founding the Romantic movement in literature.

WORKS CITED

WORKS CITED

Becker, Gary. *The Economic Approach to Human Behavior*. Chicago: Chicago University Press, 1976.

Capaldi, Nicholas. *John Stuart Mill, a Biography*. Cambridge: Cambridge University Press, 2004.

Clausen, Christopher. "John Stuart Mill's 'Very Simple Principle.'" *The Wilson Quarterly* 33.2 (2009): 40–46.

Cowling, Maurice. *Mill and Liberalism*. Cambridge: Cambridge University Press, 1963.

Donner, Wendy, and Richard A. Fumerton. *Mill*. Chichester: Wiley-Blackwell, 2009.

Eggleston, Ben, Dale E. Miller and David Weinstein, eds. *John Stuart Mill and the Art of Life*. Oxford: Oxford University Press, 2011.

Fawcett, Millicent Garrett. Introduction to *On Liberty: Representative Government; The Subjection of Women; Three Essays* by John Stuart Mill. Oxford: Oxford University Press, 1960.

Friedman, Milton. "The Methodology of Positive Economics." In *Essays in Positive Economics*. Chicago: Chicago University Press, 1953.

Hamburger, Joseph "Individuality and Moral Reform: the Rhetoric of Liberty and the Reality of Restraint in Mill's *On Liberty*" G. W. Smith, ed., *John Stuart Mill's Social and Political Thought: Critical Assessments*. London: Routledge, 1998: 405.

John Stuart Mill On Liberty and Control. Princeton: Princeton University Press, 1999.

Himmelfarb, Gertrude. Introduction to *Essays in Politics and Culture* by John Stuart Mill. New York: Doubleday and Co., 1963.

Hobbes, Thomas. *Leviathan.* 1651

Iwama, Toshihiko. "Parties, Middle-Class Voters, and the Urban Community: Rethinking the Halifax Parliamentary Borough Elections, 1832–1852." *Northern History* 51.1(2014): 91–112.

Kaplan, Robert D. "John Stuart Mill, Dead Thinker of the Year." *Foreign Policy* 190 (2011): 94–95.

Letwin, Shirley. *The Pursuit of Certainty: David Hume, Jeremy Bentham, John Stuart Mill, Beatrice Webb*. Cambridge: Cambridge University Press, 1965.

Locke, John. *Two Treatises of Government* (1689)

A Letter Concerning Toleration (1689)

Malthus, Thomas. *An Essay on the Principle of Population*. Cambridge: Cambridge University Press, 1992.

Mandelbaum, Maurice. *History, Man, and Reason: A Study in Nineteenth-Century Thought*. Baltimore: John Hopkins Press, 1971.

Mill, John Stuart. *An Early Draft of John Stuart Mill's Autobiography*. Edited by Jack Stillinger. Urbana: University of Illinois Press, 1961.

A System of Logic (1843)

Considerations on Representative Government (1861)

On Liberty. New York: Dover Publications, 2002.

On Liberty and Other Essays. Edited by John Gray. Oxford: Oxford University Press, 1998.

On Liberty: Representative Government; The Subjection of Women; Three Essays. Edited by Millicent Garrett Fawcett. Oxford: Oxford University Press, 1960.

Principles of Political Economy (1848)

The Subjection of Women. Paris: Editions Artisan Devereaux, 2014.

"The Utility of Religion." In *Three Essays on Religion: Nature, The Utility of Religion, Theism*. Amherst, NY: Prometheus Books, 1998.

Utilitarianism. (1861)

Nathanson, Stephen. "John Stuart Mill on Economic Justice and the Alleviation of Poverty." *Journal of Social Philosophy* 43.2 (2012): 161–76.

Norton, Andrew. "*On Liberty* at 150." *Policy* 25.2 (2009): 49–52.

Polanyi, Karl. *The Great Transformation: The Political and Economic Origins of Our Times*. Boston: Beacon Press, 2001.

Rawls, John. *A Theory of Justice* (1971)

Ricardo, David. *Principles of Political Economy and Taxation*. New York: Dover Publications, 1994.

Ryan, Alan. *J. S. Mill*. London and Boston: Routledge and Kegan Paul, 1974.

Sen, Amartya. "A Decade of Human Development." *Journal of Human Development* 1.1 (2000): 17–23.

Skelton, Anthony. "Liberty's godfather." *The Globe and Mail*, May 20, 2006.

Skorupski, John. *Why Read Mill Today?* London: Routledge, 2006.

Smallwood, Christine. "Back Talk: Martha C. Nussbaum." *The Nation* (2010), accessed May 10, 2015, http://www.thenation.com/article/back-talk-martha-c-nussbaum#.

Smith, Adam. *An Inquiry into the Nature and Causes of the Wealth of Nations*. Indianapolis: Liberty Fund, 1994.

Stephen, James Fitzjames. *Liberty, Equality, Fraternity and Three Brief Essays*. Chicago: Chicago University Press, 1992.

THE MACAT LIBRARY
BY DISCIPLINE

AFRICANA STUDIES

Chinua Achebe's *An Image of Africa: Racism in Conrad's Heart of Darkness*
W. E. B. Du Bois's *The Souls of Black Folk*
Zora Neale Huston's *Characteristics of Negro Expression*
Martin Luther King Jr's *Why We Can't Wait*
Toni Morrison's *Playing in the Dark: Whiteness in the American Literary Imagination*

ANTHROPOLOGY

Arjun Appadurai's *Modernity at Large: Cultural Dimensions of Globalisation*
Philippe Ariès's *Centuries of Childhood*
Franz Boas's *Race, Language and Culture*
Kim Chan & Renée Mauborgne's *Blue Ocean Strategy*
Jared Diamond's *Guns, Germs & Steel: the Fate of Human Societies*
Jared Diamond's *Collapse: How Societies Choose to Fail or Survive*
E. E. Evans-Pritchard's *Witchcraft, Oracles and Magic Among the Azande*
James Ferguson's *The Anti-Politics Machine*
Clifford Geertz's *The Interpretation of Cultures*
David Graeber's *Debt: the First 5000 Years*
Karen Ho's *Liquidated: An Ethnography of Wall Street*
Geert Hofstede's *Culture's Consequences: Comparing Values, Behaviors, Institutes and Organizations across Nations*
Claude Lévi-Strauss's *Structural Anthropology*
Jay Macleod's *Ain't No Makin' It: Aspirations and Attainment in a Low-Income Neighborhood*
Saba Mahmood's *The Politics of Piety: The Islamic Revival and the Feminist Subject*
Marcel Mauss's *The Gift*

BUSINESS

Jean Lave & Etienne Wenger's *Situated Learning*
Theodore Levitt's *Marketing Myopia*
Burton G. Malkiel's *A Random Walk Down Wall Street*
Douglas McGregor's *The Human Side of Enterprise*
Michael Porter's *Competitive Strategy: Creating and Sustaining Superior Performance*
John Kotter's *Leading Change*
C. K. Prahalad & Gary Hamel's *The Core Competence of the Corporation*

CRIMINOLOGY

Michelle Alexander's *The New Jim Crow: Mass Incarceration in the Age of Colorblindness*
Michael R. Gottfredson & Travis Hirschi's *A General Theory of Crime*
Richard Herrnstein & Charles A. Murray's *The Bell Curve: Intelligence and Class Structure in American Life*
Elizabeth Loftus's *Eyewitness Testimony*
Jay Macleod's *Ain't No Makin' It: Aspirations and Attainment in a Low-Income Neighborhood*
Philip Zimbardo's *The Lucifer Effect*

ECONOMICS

Janet Abu-Lughod's *Before European Hegemony*
Ha-Joon Chang's *Kicking Away the Ladder*
David Brion Davis's *The Problem of Slavery in the Age of Revolution*
Milton Friedman's *The Role of Monetary Policy*
Milton Friedman's *Capitalism and Freedom*
David Graeber's *Debt: the First 5000 Years*
Friedrich Hayek's *The Road to Serfdom*
Karen Ho's *Liquidated: An Ethnography of Wall Street*

John Maynard Keynes's *The General Theory of Employment, Interest and Money*
Charles P. Kindleberger's *Manias, Panics and Crashes*
Robert Lucas's *Why Doesn't Capital Flow from Rich to Poor Countries?*
Burton G. Malkiel's *A Random Walk Down Wall Street*
Thomas Robert Malthus's *An Essay on the Principle of Population*
Karl Marx's *Capital*
Thomas Piketty's *Capital in the Twenty-First Century*
Amartya Sen's *Development as Freedom*
Adam Smith's *The Wealth of Nations*
Nassim Nicholas Taleb's *The Black Swan: The Impact of the Highly Improbable*
Amos Tversky's & Daniel Kahneman's *Judgment under Uncertainty: Heuristics and Biases*
Mahbub Ul Haq's *Reflections on Human Development*
Max Weber's *The Protestant Ethic and the Spirit of Capitalism*

FEMINISM AND GENDER STUDIES

Judith Butler's *Gender Trouble*
Simone De Beauvoir's *The Second Sex*
Michel Foucault's *History of Sexuality*
Betty Friedan's *The Feminine Mystique*
Saba Mahmood's *The Politics of Piety: The Islamic Revival and the Feminist Subject*
Joan Wallach Scott's *Gender and the Politics of History*
Mary Wollstonecraft's *A Vindication of the Rights of Woman*
Virginia Woolf's *A Room of One's Own*

GEOGRAPHY

The Brundtland Report's *Our Common Future*
Rachel Carson's *Silent Spring*
Charles Darwin's *On the Origin of Species*
James Ferguson's *The Anti-Politics Machine*
Jane Jacobs's *The Death and Life of Great American Cities*
James Lovelock's *Gaia: A New Look at Life on Earth*
Amartya Sen's *Development as Freedom*
Mathis Wackernagel & William Rees's *Our Ecological Footprint*

HISTORY

Janet Abu-Lughod's *Before European Hegemony*
Benedict Anderson's *Imagined Communities*
Bernard Bailyn's *The Ideological Origins of the American Revolution*
Hanna Batatu's *The Old Social Classes And The Revolutionary Movements Of Iraq*
Christopher Browning's *Ordinary Men: Reserve Police Batallion 101 and the Final Solution in Poland*
Edmund Burke's *Reflections on the Revolution in France*
William Cronon's *Nature's Metropolis: Chicago And The Great West*
Alfred W. Crosby's *The Columbian Exchange*
Hamid Dabashi's *Iran: A People Interrupted*
David Brion Davis's *The Problem of Slavery in the Age of Revolution*
Nathalie Zemon Davis's *The Return of Martin Guerre*
Jared Diamond's *Guns, Germs & Steel: the Fate of Human Societies*
Frank Dikotter's *Mao's Great Famine*
John W Dower's *War Without Mercy: Race And Power In The Pacific War*
W. E. B. Du Bois's *The Souls of Black Folk*
Richard J. Evans's *In Defence of History*
Lucien Febvre's *The Problem of Unbelief in the 16th Century*
Sheila Fitzpatrick's *Everyday Stalinism*

Eric Foner's *Reconstruction: America's Unfinished Revolution, 1863-1877*
Michel Foucault's *Discipline and Punish*
Michel Foucault's *History of Sexuality*
Francis Fukuyama's *The End of History and the Last Man*
John Lewis Gaddis's *We Now Know: Rethinking Cold War History*
Ernest Gellner's *Nations and Nationalism*
Eugene Genovese's *Roll, Jordan, Roll: The World the Slaves Made*
Carlo Ginzburg's *The Night Battles*
Daniel Goldhagen's *Hitler's Willing Executioners*
Jack Goldstone's *Revolution and Rebellion in the Early Modern World*
Antonio Gramsci's *The Prison Notebooks*
Alexander Hamilton, John Jay & James Madison's *The Federalist Papers*
Christopher Hill's *The World Turned Upside Down*
Carole Hillenbrand's *The Crusades: Islamic Perspectives*
Thomas Hobbes's *Leviathan*
Eric Hobsbawm's *The Age Of Revolution*
John A. Hobson's *Imperialism: A Study*
Albert Hourani's *History of the Arab Peoples*
Samuel P. Huntington's *The Clash of Civilizations and the Remaking of World Order*
C. L. R. James's *The Black Jacobins*
Tony Judt's *Postwar: A History of Europe Since 1945*
Ernst Kantorowicz's *The King's Two Bodies: A Study in Medieval Political Theology*
Paul Kennedy's *The Rise and Fall of the Great Powers*
Ian Kershaw's *The "Hitler Myth": Image and Reality in the Third Reich*
John Maynard Keynes's *The General Theory of Employment, Interest and Money*
Charles P. Kindleberger's *Manias, Panics and Crashes*
Martin Luther King Jr's *Why We Can't Wait*
Henry Kissinger's *World Order: Reflections on the Character of Nations and the Course of History*
Thomas Kuhn's *The Structure of Scientific Revolutions*
Georges Lefebvre's *The Coming of the French Revolution*
John Locke's *Two Treatises of Government*
Niccolò Machiavelli's *The Prince*
Thomas Robert Malthus's *An Essay on the Principle of Population*
Mahmood Mamdani's *Citizen and Subject: Contemporary Africa And The Legacy Of Late Colonialism*
Karl Marx's *Capital*
Stanley Milgram's *Obedience to Authority*
John Stuart Mill's *On Liberty*
Thomas Paine's *Common Sense*
Thomas Paine's *Rights of Man*
Geoffrey Parker's *Global Crisis: War, Climate Change and Catastrophe in the Seventeenth Century*
Jonathan Riley-Smith's *The First Crusade and the Idea of Crusading*
Jean-Jacques Rousseau's *The Social Contract*
Joan Wallach Scott's *Gender and the Politics of History*
Theda Skocpol's *States and Social Revolutions*
Adam Smith's *The Wealth of Nations*
Timothy Snyder's *Bloodlands: Europe Between Hitler and Stalin*
Sun Tzu's *The Art of War*
Keith Thomas's *Religion and the Decline of Magic*
Thucydides's *The History of the Peloponnesian War*
Frederick Jackson Turner's *The Significance of the Frontier in American History*
Odd Arne Westad's *The Global Cold War: Third World Interventions And The Making Of Our Times*

The Macat Library By Discipline

LITERATURE

Chinua Achebe's *An Image of Africa: Racism in Conrad's Heart of Darkness*
Roland Barthes's *Mythologies*
Homi K. Bhabha's *The Location of Culture*
Judith Butler's *Gender Trouble*
Simone De Beauvoir's *The Second Sex*
Ferdinand De Saussure's *Course in General Linguistics*
T. S. Eliot's *The Sacred Wood: Essays on Poetry and Criticism*
Zora Neale Huston's *Characteristics of Negro Expression*
Toni Morrison's *Playing in the Dark: Whiteness in the American Literary Imagination*
Edward Said's *Orientalism*
Gayatri Chakravorty Spivak's *Can the Subaltern Speak?*
Mary Wollstonecraft's *A Vindication of the Rights of Women*
Virginia Woolf's *A Room of One's Own*

PHILOSOPHY

Elizabeth Anscombe's *Modern Moral Philosophy*
Hannah Arendt's *The Human Condition*
Aristotle's *Metaphysics*
Aristotle's *Nicomachean Ethics*
Edmund Gettier's *Is Justified True Belief Knowledge?*
Georg Wilhelm Friedrich Hegel's *Phenomenology of Spirit*
David Hume's *Dialogues Concerning Natural Religion*
David Hume's *The Enquiry for Human Understanding*
Immanuel Kant's *Religion within the Boundaries of Mere Reason*
Immanuel Kant's *Critique of Pure Reason*
Søren Kierkegaard's *The Sickness Unto Death*
Søren Kierkegaard's *Fear and Trembling*
C. S. Lewis's *The Abolition of Man*
Alasdair MacIntyre's *After Virtue*
Marcus Aurelius's *Meditations*
Friedrich Nietzsche's *On the Genealogy of Morality*
Friedrich Nietzsche's *Beyond Good and Evil*
Plato's *Republic*
Plato's *Symposium*
Jean-Jacques Rousseau's *The Social Contract*
Gilbert Ryle's *The Concept of Mind*
Baruch Spinoza's *Ethics*
Sun Tzu's *The Art of War*
Ludwig Wittgenstein's *Philosophical Investigations*

POLITICS

Benedict Anderson's *Imagined Communities*
Aristotle's *Politics*
Bernard Bailyn's *The Ideological Origins of the American Revolution*
Edmund Burke's *Reflections on the Revolution in France*
John C. Calhoun's *A Disquisition on Government*
Ha-Joon Chang's *Kicking Away the Ladder*
Hamid Dabashi's *Iran: A People Interrupted*
Hamid Dabashi's *Theology of Discontent: The Ideological Foundation of the Islamic Revolution in Iran*
Robert Dahl's *Democracy and its Critics*
Robert Dahl's *Who Governs?*
David Brion Davis's *The Problem of Slavery in the Age of Revolution*

Alexis De Tocqueville's *Democracy in America*
James Ferguson's *The Anti-Politics Machine*
Frank Dikotter's *Mao's Great Famine*
Sheila Fitzpatrick's *Everyday Stalinism*
Eric Foner's *Reconstruction: America's Unfinished Revolution, 1863-1877*
Milton Friedman's *Capitalism and Freedom*
Francis Fukuyama's *The End of History and the Last Man*
John Lewis Gaddis's *We Now Know: Rethinking Cold War History*
Ernest Gellner's *Nations and Nationalism*
David Graeber's *Debt: the First 5000 Years*
Antonio Gramsci's *The Prison Notebooks*
Alexander Hamilton, John Jay & James Madison's *The Federalist Papers*
Friedrich Hayek's *The Road to Serfdom*
Christopher Hill's *The World Turned Upside Down*
Thomas Hobbes's *Leviathan*
John A. Hobson's *Imperialism: A Study*
Samuel P. Huntington's *The Clash of Civilizations and the Remaking of World Order*
Tony Judt's *Postwar: A History of Europe Since 1945*
David C. Kang's *China Rising: Peace, Power and Order in East Asia*
Paul Kennedy's *The Rise and Fall of Great Powers*
Robert Keohane's *After Hegemony*
Martin Luther King Jr.'s *Why We Can't Wait*
Henry Kissinger's *World Order: Reflections on the Character of Nations and the Course of History*
John Locke's *Two Treatises of Government*
Niccolò Machiavelli's *The Prince*
Thomas Robert Malthus's *An Essay on the Principle of Population*
Mahmood Mamdani's *Citizen and Subject: Contemporary Africa And The Legacy Of Late Colonialism*
Karl Marx's *Capital*
John Stuart Mill's *On Liberty*
John Stuart Mill's *Utilitarianism*
Hans Morgenthau's *Politics Among Nations*
Thomas Paine's *Common Sense*
Thomas Paine's *Rights of Man*
Thomas Piketty's *Capital in the Twenty-First Century*
Robert D. Putman's *Bowling Alone*
John Rawls's *Theory of Justice*
Jean-Jacques Rousseau's *The Social Contract*
Theda Skocpol's *States and Social Revolutions*
Adam Smith's *The Wealth of Nations*
Sun Tzu's *The Art of War*
Henry David Thoreau's *Civil Disobedience*
Thucydides's *The History of the Peloponnesian War*
Kenneth Waltz's *Theory of International Politics*
Max Weber's *Politics as a Vocation*
Odd Arne Westad's *The Global Cold War: Third World Interventions And The Making Of Our Times*

POSTCOLONIAL STUDIES

Roland Barthes's *Mythologies*
Frantz Fanon's *Black Skin, White Masks*
Homi K. Bhabha's *The Location of Culture*
Gustavo Gutiérrez's *A Theology of Liberation*
Edward Said's *Orientalism*
Gayatri Chakravorty Spivak's *Can the Subaltern Speak?*

The Macat Library By Discipline

PSYCHOLOGY

Gordon Allport's *The Nature of Prejudice*
Alan Baddeley & Graham Hitch's *Aggression: A Social Learning Analysis*
Albert Bandura's *Aggression: A Social Learning Analysis*
Leon Festinger's *A Theory of Cognitive Dissonance*
Sigmund Freud's *The Interpretation of Dreams*
Betty Friedan's *The Feminine Mystique*
Michael R. Gottfredson & Travis Hirschi's *A General Theory of Crime*
Eric Hoffer's *The True Believer: Thoughts on the Nature of Mass Movements*
William James's *Principles of Psychology*
Elizabeth Loftus's *Eyewitness Testimony*
A. H. Maslow's *A Theory of Human Motivation*
Stanley Milgram's *Obedience to Authority*
Steven Pinker's *The Better Angels of Our Nature*
Oliver Sacks's *The Man Who Mistook His Wife For a Hat*
Richard Thaler & Cass Sunstein's *Nudge: Improving Decisions About Health, Wealth and Happiness*
Amos Tversky's *Judgment under Uncertainty: Heuristics and Biases*
Philip Zimbardo's *The Lucifer Effect*

SCIENCE

Rachel Carson's *Silent Spring*
William Cronon's *Nature's Metropolis: Chicago And The Great West*
Alfred W. Crosby's *The Columbian Exchange*
Charles Darwin's *On the Origin of Species*
Richard Dawkin's *The Selfish Gene*
Thomas Kuhn's *The Structure of Scientific Revolutions*
Geoffrey Parker's *Global Crisis: War, Climate Change and Catastrophe in the Seventeenth Century*
Mathis Wackernagel & William Rees's *Our Ecological Footprint*

SOCIOLOGY

Michelle Alexander's *The New Jim Crow: Mass Incarceration in the Age of Colorblindness*
Gordon Allport's *The Nature of Prejudice*
Albert Bandura's *Aggression: A Social Learning Analysis*
Hanna Batatu's *The Old Social Classes And The Revolutionary Movements Of Iraq*
Ha-Joon Chang's *Kicking Away the Ladder*
W. E. B. Du Bois's *The Souls of Black Folk*
Émile Durkheim's *On Suicide*
Frantz Fanon's *Black Skin, White Masks*
Frantz Fanon's *The Wretched of the Earth*
Eric Foner's *Reconstruction: America's Unfinished Revolution, 1863-1877*
Eugene Genovese's *Roll, Jordan, Roll: The World the Slaves Made*
Jack Goldstone's *Revolution and Rebellion in the Early Modern World*
Antonio Gramsci's *The Prison Notebooks*
Richard Herrnstein & Charles A Murray's *The Bell Curve: Intelligence and Class Structure in American Life*
Eric Hoffer's *The True Believer: Thoughts on the Nature of Mass Movements*
Jane Jacobs's *The Death and Life of Great American Cities*
Robert Lucas's *Why Doesn't Capital Flow from Rich to Poor Countries?*
Jay Macleod's *Ain't No Makin' It: Aspirations and Attainment in a Low Income Neighborhood*
Elaine May's *Homeward Bound: American Families in the Cold War Era*
Douglas McGregor's *The Human Side of Enterprise*
C. Wright Mills's *The Sociological Imagination*

Thomas Piketty's *Capital in the Twenty-First Century*
Robert D. Putman's *Bowling Alone*
David Riesman's *The Lonely Crowd: A Study of the Changing American Character*
Edward Said's *Orientalism*
Joan Wallach Scott's *Gender and the Politics of History*
Theda Skocpol's *States and Social Revolutions*
Max Weber's *The Protestant Ethic and the Spirit of Capitalism*

THEOLOGY

Augustine's *Confessions*
Benedict's *Rule of St Benedict*
Gustavo Gutiérrez's *A Theology of Liberation*
Carole Hillenbrand's *The Crusades: Islamic Perspectives*
David Hume's *Dialogues Concerning Natural Religion*
Immanuel Kant's *Religion within the Boundaries of Mere Reason*
Ernst Kantorowicz's *The King's Two Bodies: A Study in Medieval Political Theology*
Søren Kierkegaard's *The Sickness Unto Death*
C. S. Lewis's *The Abolition of Man*
Saba Mahmood's *The Politics of Piety: The Islamic Revival and the Feminist Subject*
Baruch Spinoza's *Ethics*
Keith Thomas's *Religion and the Decline of Magic*

COMING SOON

Chris Argyris's *The Individual and the Organisation*
Seyla Benhabib's *The Rights of Others*
Walter Benjamin's *The Work Of Art in the Age of Mechanical Reproduction*
John Berger's *Ways of Seeing*
Pierre Bourdieu's *Outline of a Theory of Practice*
Mary Douglas's *Purity and Danger*
Roland Dworkin's *Taking Rights Seriously*
James G. March's *Exploration and Exploitation in Organisational Learning*
Ikujiro Nonaka's *A Dynamic Theory of Organizational Knowledge Creation*
Griselda Pollock's *Vision and Difference*
Amartya Sen's *Inequality Re-Examined*
Susan Sontag's *On Photography*
Yasser Tabbaa's *The Transformation of Islamic Art*
Ludwig von Mises's *Theory of Money and Credit*